Things ABOVE

Cultivating a Passionate Pursuit of God

MARK G. TROTTER

Copyright © 2021 by Mark G. Trotter. All scripture quotations are taken from the King James Authorized Version.

First published in 2021 by Living Faith Books.

All rights reserved. This book or parts thereof may not be reproduced in any form, stored in any retrieval system, or transmitted in any form by any means—electronic, mechanical, photocopy, recording, or otherwise—without prior written permission of the publisher and/or author, except as provided by United States of America copyright law.

Living Faith Books
3953 Walnut St
Kansas City, MO 64111

Creative Director: Joel Springer
Cover Art: Havilah Guenther
Chief Editor: Melissa Wharton
Page Editing: Anna Ryan
ISBN: 978-1-950004-11-9
Printed in the United States of America

Contents

Introduction	7
1 - Leaving Your First Love	11
2 - Risen with Christ	17
3 - Things Above / Things On the Earth	23
4 - Passionately Pursuing God	29
5 - That I May Know Him	35
6 - No Place of Departure	41
7 - Family in Heaven	49
8 - The Wrong Passions	53
9 - The Simple Life	59
10 - A Fly on the Prison Wall	67
11 - Not I, but Christ	75
12 - Better Off Dead	81

Introduction

Have you ever been handed a lukewarm mug of coffee on a cold winter day? It doesn't quite hit the spot, does it? What you really wanted was a piping hot drink to warm yourself up, but instead you got something that wasn't even cold and refreshing — just room temperature and disgusting.

That very concept of lukewarmness is what characterizes the church in today's age. Revelation chapters 2-3 contain letters from Jesus Christ Himself to seven churches to both commend and admonish them. Because the Bible has three main applications — historical, doctrinal, and devotional — each part of scripture applies in some way not only to the time it was written, but to believers throughout history as well (including us today). We can understand these letters in Revelation 2-3 historically as literal communication between God and those churches in 95 AD, but we can also understand them as a template for interpreting church history.

As we trace the church throughout history, we find that those things Jesus discussed in Revelation 2-3 provide a perfect outline of all that's taken place in the history of Christianity. We see the faithfulness of the early church, the persecution believers began to face, the false doctrines that began to creep in, the revivals that took place, and the apathy that is so characteristic of Christianity today. And as we look closely at history, we see that we entered into what's often called the Laodicean church age around the beginning of the 20th century. In Revelation 3:14-18, we read about God's perspective of believers both at the Laodicean church thousands of years ago and believers in the church today. You'll see that there is quite a scathing rebuke of the church in these verses which ties back to the temperature of their heart: they were woefully lukewarm.

Having pastored in five of the thirteen decades that have comprised the Laodicean church period thus far (1900 – present), I can tell you that if there

Introduction

is one arena in which people in Laodicea have struggled big time, it is with relationships. They struggle in their relationships with their spouses. They struggle in their relationships with their parents and children. They struggle in relationships at work. They struggle in relationships with lost people. And they even struggle in relationships with those who are saved and part of their own local church.

But there's one singular reason Laodiceans have struggled in all of these relationships, and that's because we struggle to know how to have a relationship with God! We've become lukewarm in our pursuit of Him, and it reaches out into every part of our lives.

It turns out that all of these relationships just happen to be what Paul addresses in the practical section of the book of Colossians (chapters 3 and 4). Here's an outline of this practical section:

Our relationship with... God (3:1-17)
　　　　　　　　　　... our spouse (3:18-19)
　　　　　　　　　　... our parents/children (3:20-21)
　　　　　　　　　　... those at work (3:22-4:1)
　　　　　　　　　　... the lost (4:2-6)
　　　　　　　　　　... the saved (4:7-18)

Notice that the longest of these sections is about our relationship with God! This tells us that the foundation for all our earthly relationships has to be our heavenly one!

If we could get that relationship right, families that seem to be plagued with many insurmountable, complicated, and confusing issues could be resolved with one simple piece of counsel to wives (3:18); one simple piece of counsel to husbands (3:19); one simple piece of counsel to children (3:20); and one simple piece of counsel to fathers (3:21). If you have ever been involved in counseling marital and parental issues in Laodicea, the idea that if every individual just did one simple thing to rectify the problems seems ludicrous, even laughable!

Remember, however, that this counsel comes <u>after</u> presuming that we are living out the first 17 verses of Colossians 3, as God reveals what our lives ought to look like now that we've been saved (i.e. "risen with Christ"— Col 3:1, 2:12). The content in the book of Colossians is particularly relevant to us Laodiceans because in verse 16 of the last chapter, Paul tells them to swap letters with the Laodiceans! What was important for the Colossians to read was also important for the Laodiceans to read. In our age, therefore, I believe that the biblical concepts held in this passage of Colossians are some of the most important for us to grasp.

What he covers in those 17 verses reaches deep into all the other relationships we have in our lives. All our relationships are designed *by* God to be built upon and flow out of the relationship that we have *with* God. Only when we are living in the simplicity of the first 17 verses of chapter three can we be brought back to the simplicity of the statements regarding the other relationships in our lives.

That's the intention of this book: to examine those 17 verses and lay out exactly what a relationship with God is supposed to look like according to God's word. I hope that as you see these simple truths from scripture, you are able to take hold of a simple, fruitful, passionate walk with Christ and transformed relationships with others.

Chapter 1

Leaving Your First Love

It happened in the great church of Ephesus right around the end of the first century. A lot of great things were happening in the church. They knew WHAT they believed and WHY they believed it, and they were zealous enough to stand against anyone that taught something other than sound doctrine. They were hard-working people. They knew what it meant to serve the Lord, and they persevered — even through tough times and adversity.

Those are characteristics of a great church! Would to God that all of those things we just talked about could be said of every church, including your own! I mean, those are some pretty phenomenal qualities, and we know that those were the actual characteristics present in that church because of the things our Lord addressed to them in a letter transcribed by the Apostle John in Revelation 2:1-7. He said to John, "Unto the angel of the church of Ephesus write…"

> "These things saith he that holdeth the seven stars in his right hand, who walketh in the midst of the seven golden candlesticks; 2 I know thy works, and thy labour, and thy patience, and how thou canst not bear them which are evil: and thou hast tried them which say they are apostles, and are not, and hast found them liars: 3 And hast borne, and hast patience, and for my name's sake hast laboured, and hast not fainted."

That's a great church! I don't know many pastors who wouldn't love for those things to be said about their local church, especially if it was the Lord Jesus Christ Himself saying it!

But somehow, in the midst of all those wonderful things that were happening, something tragic had begun to take place. Something that broke the Lord's

Chapter 1

heart. Look at what He told them in the very next verse after commending them so positively in the previous verses. Jesus said,

> "Nevertheless I have somewhat against thee, because thou hast left thy first love." (Rev 2:4)

Wow! What a statement! Somehow in the midst of faithfully serving the Lord, uncompromisingly holding to His Word, and contending for the faith, this church had drifted away from the very thing that had prompted all of that tremendous activity in the first place... Jesus! They had "left their first love." In other words, they had LEFT the LOVE they had for Him when they FIRST entered their relationship with Him.

But something you need to make sure you see is that though this tragic thing that Jesus identified had happened to their inward love for Him, all of the outward activity in their church was still in full operation.

But now, rather than being caught up with the Lord Jesus, they had become caught up in the machinery of ministry. Yes, they were still mightily involved in the <u>work of the Lord</u>, but had left the <u>Lord of the work</u>! They were still holding tenaciously to the <u>word of God</u>, but had left the <u>God of the word</u>. What an unbelievably sad statement our Lord makes to this church:

> "Thou hast left thy first love."

Now wait, I thought this book was supposed to focus on Colossians! Why are we starting off with all this talk about Ephesus? Don't worry, I haven't forgotten! But this concept of leaving our first love is intertwined with the concepts we'll be looking at. And not only is this concept intertwined, but the books of Colossians and Ephesians (written to the church at Ephesus, obviously!) are as well. Paul's letter to the Ephesians and his letter to the Colossians are often referred to as twin epistles (letters). In other words, these two letters basically follow the same track — that is, they cover the same basic subject matter. But they do so from a slightly different standpoint so that they complement each other, which we'll see more about in the next chapter. So, as we read on about Christ's words to Ephesus, keep this connection in mind.

Now, look — I'm recounting all of these things that happened in the church of Ephesus because the same thing that happens to churches happens to individuals, "of whom I am chief" (1 Ti 1:15).

Leaving Your First Love

We can be cruising along in our Christian life with no blatant, horrific, deep-seated sin that we're involved in or excusing. We can have a daily quiet time... we can be faithful to all of the services at the church... we can even have a place of service where we've proven ourselves to be faithful! We can seek to hold to the truth of the word of God and to share it with others when we have opportunity. But in the midst of all of these wonderful (and really, I do mean wonderful!) things that are true of our lives by the working of His grace, some of us know that if Jesus were to dictate a letter to us, after commending us for these things, He would say to us that dreadful "nevertheless":

> "Nevertheless I have somewhat against thee, because thou hast left thy first love."

As you're reading this today, is that what you hear Him saying to you?

If that's not what He needs to say to you, praise the Lord! What an awesome testimony of His grace, power, and working in your life! But, for many others of us, the question is: Can we and will we be honest enough with ourselves, and honest enough with the Lord — who already knows the truth about our hearts — to be able to say...

"Yeah, that's me! I have left my first love. I remember when love was new, the love and passion that used to burn in my heart for the Lord Jesus Christ (Psa 42:1-2). I remember the longing in my heart to know His word (Php 3:10)... the hunger and thirst in my soul for intimate fellowship with Him (Psa 63:1-2)... the groaning in the deepest recesses of my being for this body to experience its redemption (Rom 8:22-23) so I could be freed from the very presence of sin!

"But, I find myself no longer burning, longing, hungering, thirsting, or groaning. There is a complacency that has somehow crept into my life. My Christian life has become sort of automatic. I know I'm not *cold* to the Lord or the things of the Lord, but I also know I'm not *hot*. I probably wouldn't have thought it last night before I went to bed, but I think that qualifies me as (gulp!) lukewarm."

Look at what Jesus wrote in His letter to the church of the Laodiceans in Revelation 3:15-16...

> "I know thy works, that thou art neither cold nor hot: I would thou wert

Chapter 1

cold or hot. 16 So then because thou art lukewarm, and neither cold nor hot, I will spue thee out of my mouth."

Is that where you find yourself today? If so, know that there is good news even in the midst of that difficult realization. Notice that Jesus didn't say, "You lost your first love." He said, "You left it." That's not just semantics! There's a big difference between LOST and LEFT! Most of us can probably best relate to that in terms of our wallet. There's a vast difference between losing your wallet and leaving it. When it's LOST, the chances of getting it back are mighty slim. I mean, where do you even begin? But if you LEFT it, yeah, there is certainly some effort involved, but you aren't left with the feeling of helplessness and hopelessness that you have when it's LOST. You just go back to where you LEFT it, get it, and then get going!

You see, that's why Jesus didn't use the word *lost*. Yes, He certainly wants to get your attention today, and He certainly wants you to identify where you really are spiritually, but He doesn't want you to be overcome with feelings of helplessness and hopelessness! He wants you to be able to get that "first love" passion back!

As we saw in the introduction, part of the reason a study of Colossians is so relevant to us Laodiceans is because God, through Paul, commanded the churches at Colosse and Laodicea to swap and read each other's epistles. If Laodicea's problem is that they're lukewarm in their love towards Christ, then the solution is to refocus their heart! To once again seek the things they ought to seek and set their affection on the things they ought to be affectionate towards — that's what this book is all about.

Oh, I hope and pray that every person reading this book will humble themselves before the Lord today, crying out to God that He would help us to be brought back to experience our "first love" with Him, crying out for Him to restore to us the joy of His salvation (Psa 51:12). That, in the same way we did when we got saved, He would bring us back to hunger and thirst, not only for His righteousness (Mat 5:6), but for Him! (Psa 63:1-2)

But where does the process of getting back our "first love" passion for Christ even begin? Let me assure you of this: my thoughts, words, or insights in this book cannot bring back that passion, that hunger, or that thirst! If I had the ability to flip that switch in you, I'd flip it. But that switch is your heart, and the only one who can get it to flip is you!

You say, "Well, how do I flip that switch of my heart?" Let me share with you a key principle that I learned years ago reading *The Pursuit of God* by A. W. Tozer. In those times we find ourselves without the passion for Christ that we once had, Tozer said that hungering and thirsting for Him won't just suddenly appear. You can't force that switch to flip. You probably won't end this chapter hungering and thirsting for God. But that's okay, because it doesn't begin there. It begins with <u>hungering to be hungry</u>! And it begins with <u>thirsting to be thirsty</u>! That IS something you can do today! THAT is a switch you can flip!

In your next quiet time with the Lord (maybe right now!), would you spend part of it crying out to Him that He would, indeed, cause you to hunger to be hungry and thirst to be thirsty? Once you've poured out your heart to Him concerning that, would you take the time to pray through some of the verses I've mentioned in this chapter? I've listed them for you below.

> Revelation 2:4 Nevertheless I have somewhat against thee, because thou hast left thy first love.
>
> Psalm 51:12 Restore unto me the joy of thy salvation; and uphold me with thy free spirit.
>
> Psalm 42:1-2 As the hart panteth after the water brooks, so panteth my soul after thee, O God. 2 My soul thirsteth for God, for the living God: when shall I come and appear before God?
>
> Philippians 3:10 That I may know him, and the power of his resurrection, and the fellowship of his sufferings, being made conformable unto his death;
>
> Psalm 63:1-2 O God, thou art my God; early will I seek thee: my soul thirsteth for thee, my flesh longeth for thee in a dry and thirsty land, where no water is; 2 To see thy power and thy glory, so as I have seen thee in the sanctuary.
>
> Romans 8:22-23 For we know that the whole creation groaneth and travaileth in pain together until now. 23 And not only they, but ourselves also, which have the firstfruits of the Spirit, even we ourselves groan within ourselves, waiting for the adoption, to wit, the redemption of our body.

Chapter 2

Risen with Christ

There are some key passages in the word of God that rock my world in terms of stirring my passion for God. We looked at one of them in the last chapter; Revelation 2:4 serves as a constant reminder to me of how easy it is to get into a spiritual groove and have all of the right things seemingly in place, but to have my love for Him not really be the passion that fuels all of the activity.

There are other verses that God has consistently used to remind me of what true passion for Him really looks like.

I hear David crying out to God in...

> Psalm 42:1 As the hart panteth after the water brooks, so panteth my soul after thee, O God. 2 My soul thirsteth for God, for the living God: when shall I come and appear before God?

> Psalm 63:1 O God, thou art my God; early will I seek thee: my soul thirsteth for thee, my flesh longeth for thee in a dry and thirsty land, where no water is; 2 To see thy power and thy glory, so as I have seen thee in the sanctuary. 3 Because thy lovingkindness is better than life, my lips shall praise thee. 4 Thus will I bless thee while I live: I will lift up my hands in thy name. 5 My soul shall be satisfied as with marrow and fatness; and my mouth shall praise thee with joyful lips: 6 When I remember thee upon my bed, and meditate on thee in the night watches. 7 Because thou hast been my help, therefore in the shadow of thy wings will I rejoice. 8 My soul followeth hard after thee: thy right hand upholdeth me.

Chapter 2

> Psalm 84:2 My soul longeth, yea, even fainteth for the courts of the LORD: my heart and my flesh crieth out for the living God.
>
> Psalm 143:6 I stretch forth my hands unto thee: my soul thirsteth after thee, as a thirsty land. Selah.
>
> Psalm 27:8 When thou saidst, Seek ye my face; my heart said unto thee, Thy face, LORD, will I seek.

I hear Job crying out concerning God in...

> Job 23:10 But he knoweth the way that I take: when he hath tried me, I shall come forth as gold. 11 My foot hath held his steps, his way have I kept, and not declined. 12 Neither have I gone back from the commandment of his lips; I have esteemed the words of his mouth more than my necessary food.

I hear Jeremiah crying out to God in...

> Jeremiah 15:16 Thy words were found, and I did eat them; and thy word was unto me the joy and rejoicing of mine heart: for I am called by thy name, O LORD God of hosts.

I don't know what happens to your heart as you read those verses, but God uses them to jolt me, to arrest the attention of my heart and my soul. I find myself crying out with these men, "Yeah! Me too, God! That's what I want my heart to constantly be saying to You. I want that kind of passion for You!"

Again, I think those are just some awesome verses in terms of STIRRING our passion for God! But I know of no other passage in all of the word of God that I believe does a better job of FOCUSING that passion for Him and that teaches the essentials for SUSTAINING that passion for the long haul than Colossians 3:1-17. As you read in the introduction, this passage will be the framework for the rest of this book.

Let's take a minute to hear what God says in this passage and to see where we'll be heading. Now, try not to get in a rush as you read this, but rather "study to be quiet" (1 Th 4:11). Join David in saying, "I will meditate in thy precepts, and have respect unto thy ways....My hands also will I lift up unto thy commandments, which I have loved; and I will meditate in thy statutes," and "Open thou mine eyes, that I may behold wondrous things out of thy law" (Psa 119:15, 48, 18). Here we go:

Colossians 3:1-17
1 If ye then be risen with Christ, seek those things which are above, where Christ sitteth on the right hand of God.
2 Set your affection on things above, not on things on the earth.
3 For ye are dead, and your life is hid with Christ in God.
4 When Christ, who is our life, shall appear, then shall ye also appear with him in glory
5 Mortify therefore your members which are upon the earth; fornication, uncleanness, inordinate affection, evil concupiscence, and covetousness, which is idolatry:
6 For which things' sake the wrath of God cometh on the children of disobedience:
7 In the which ye also walked some time, when ye lived in them.
8 But now ye also put off all these; anger, wrath, malice, blasphemy, filthy communication out of your mouth.
9 Lie not one to another, seeing that ye have put off the old man with his deeds;
10 And have put on the new man, which is renewed in knowledge after the image of him that created him:
11 Where there is neither Greek nor Jew, circumcision nor uncircumcision, Barbarian, Scythian, bond nor free: but Christ is all, and in all.
12 Put on therefore, as the elect of God, holy and beloved, bowels of mercies, kindness, humbleness of mind, meekness, longsuffering;
13 Forbearing one another, and forgiving one another, if any man have a quarrel against any: even as Christ forgave you, so also do ye.
14 And above all these things put on charity, which is the bond of perfectness.
15 And let the peace of God rule in your hearts, to the which also ye are called in one body; and be ye thankful.
16 Let the word of Christ dwell in you richly in all wisdom; teaching and admonishing one another in psalms and hymns and spiritual songs, singing with grace in your hearts to the Lord.
17 And whatsoever ye do in word or deed, do all in the name of the Lord Jesus, giving thanks to God and the Father by him.

Alright now, let's dive on in.

Chapter 2

First of all, let's set the context. Paul does that in the first seven words of the passage:

"If ye then be risen with Christ..."

Now, had we already been studying the first two chapters of Colossians, we would already know exactly what Paul was talking about when he referred to our being "risen with Christ." He taught the principle doctrinally back in verse 2:12, when in reference to what happened to us at salvation, he said,

"Buried with him in baptism, wherein also ye are risen with him through the faith of the operation of God, who hath raised him from the dead."

This is so important, and so exciting! But to really get it, you're going to have to engage both your mind and your heart, so be very attentive...

Paul is talking here about that time when you and I were calling upon the name of the Lord to save us (Rom 10:10-13). A time that, though we certainly didn't realize it or even have the spiritual software to comprehend it, the Spirit of God was actually "baptizing" ("immersing") us spiritually INTO Christ (1Co 12:13, Rom 6:3-5). Oh my, what a tremendous truth! The New Testament teaching that we are now "in Christ" is one of the most mind-boggling, far-reaching, life-changing concepts in all of the word of God! But here's what I want you to see: we are SAVED as a result of the Spirit of God BAPTIZING us spiritually INTO CHRIST.

The way it shakes out biblically is this: as we all know, the gospel is defined very simply as the death, burial, and resurrection of Christ (1Co 15:1-4). But the death, burial, and resurrection of Christ itself actually saves no one. What I'm saying is this: the death, burial, and resurrection of Christ provides the OPPORTUNITY for every person to be saved, but it doesn't save them. That's where FAITH comes in!

Hebrews 4:2 For unto us was the gospel preached, as well as unto them: but the word preached did not profit them, <u>not being mixed with faith in them that heard it.</u>

Ephesians 2:8-9 For by grace are ye saved <u>through faith</u>; and that not of yourselves: it is the gift of God: 9 Not of works, lest any man should boast.

Ephesians 1:12-14 That we should be to the praise of his glory, who first trusted in Christ. 13 In whom ye also trusted, after that ye heard the word of truth, the gospel of your salvation: in whom also <u>after that ye believed</u>, ye were sealed with that holy Spirit of promise, 14 Which is the earnest of our inheritance until the redemption of the purchased possession, unto the praise of his glory.

When, by faith, we call upon the name of the Lord Jesus Christ to save us, the power of the gospel is unleashed by the Spirit of God as He spiritually places us into Christ's death, and we die with Him. He then takes us and places us into His burial, and we are buried with Him. And, praise the Lord, He places us into His resurrection, and we are risen with Him! That's what Paul is talking about in Colossians 2:12! We died with Christ, we were buried with Him, and now Paul says at the end of verse 12 that the power that raised Christ from the dead is the same exact power that raised us from the spiritual death the moment we expressed FAITH in Him!

I mean, are you hearing that? Think of the incredible power that God unleashed when He reached into that tomb on the first day of the week and raised Christ from the dead. The most incredible power in the entire universe! The very power of Almighty God! THAT, my friend, is the same incredible power, in all of its fullness, that God Himself unleashed on the day we called upon His name and He reached down into the tomb of our life and raised us from the dead!

Hallelujah to ya! I'm telling you — if that there don't light your fire, your wood's wet! THAT'S what Paul is referring to in Colossians 3:1 when He says, "If ye then be risen with Christ…"

Do you see what a wallop those seven words actually pack? Do you see why we needed to spend so much time on that? The point is this: the POWER of God that raised us from the dead and to new life in Him now wants to EMPOWER us to PASSIONATELY SEEK HIM!

Oh, could I ask you to let the truth of Colossians 3:1-2 sink down into your heart and into every fiber of your being today? Pray today that God will use His word to ignite in you that passion for Him.

Chapter 3

Things Above / Things On the Earth

Oh, what unbelievable power God unleashed upon our life the very moment we called upon His name to save us! As we learned in the previous chapter from Colossians 2:12, the power that God exercised to raise our Lord Jesus Christ from the dead physically is the same power that God put into operation that raised you and me from the dead spiritually! It was the power of resurrection, the most powerful force in the universe. But not only is that the power that saved us, that's the power that now resides in us. For God's glory's sake, don't ever allow yourself to underestimate or trivialize the power of the salvation you've received!

There's another incredible dimension that God reveals to us about what it means to be "risen with Christ" in Ephesians 2. Remember from chapter one how we saw that Ephesians and Colossians are twin epistles? Well, when you place the contents of each letter next to each other, you begin to see how they dovetail into a beautiful, harmonious oneness that provides incredible clarity and understanding. Such is the case with our being "risen with Christ."

Paul says in Colossians 2:12...

> "Buried with him in baptism, wherein also ye are risen with him through the faith of the operation of God, who hath raised him from the dead."

And he says in Ephesians 2:4-6...

> "But God, who is rich in mercy, for his great love wherewith he loved us, Even when we were dead in sins, hath quickened us together with Christ, (by grace ye are saved;) And hath raised us up together, and made us sit together in heavenly places in Christ Jesus:"

Chapter 3

Now, here's the way these verses dovetail together: Colossians 2:12 teaches us about the TYPE of power God put into operation when He raised us from the dead. Ephesians 2:6 teaches us about the RESULT of that power being put into operation. When we put the two teachings together, we find God is saying that the power that raised Christ from the dead is the power that raised us out of our spiritual death. But when God exercised that power, He also raised us spiritually into the very throne room of heaven, and we are (present tense!) seated with Christ in heaven.

Now, I don't want to get too many things going here, but I can't help but mention that nobody who really understands the spiritual realities taught in the book of Ephesians could ever wrestle with the false teaching that a person could lose their salvation! No, when a person is saved, God immediately raises them spiritually to be seated with Him in heavenly places. We are as good as there!

Now, I don't presume to fully comprehend just how it is that you are seated wherever you happen to be reading this right now, and yet, at the very same time, you are also seated with Christ in heaven. Yeah, that's a little hard to totally get my mind wrapped around, but it doesn't change the fact that I believe it! The fact is, we believe a lot of things we don't understand. I don't understand how I flip a switch in my kitchen and "in a moment, in the twinkling of an eye" as it were, an electrical current races from the switch to a light fixture in the ceiling and illuminates the room. But I still believe it! So as mind-boggling as it is, the fact is that at this very second, you and I are living in a physical body on the earth and yet at the same time are actually SEATED with Christ in heaven as citizens of His heavenly kingdom (Eph 2:19, Php 3:20).

Wow! Powerful stuff! And when you begin to understand the actual power that saved us and the powerful implications of what that really means, the most natural question in all the world is: What ought the resurrection life of Jesus actually look like in the life of someone who has become a recipient of it?

That's exactly the question Paul beelines to answer as soon as he wraps up the doctrinal section of Colossians in chapters 1 and 2. He gets to chapter 3 and says...

> "If ye then be risen with Christ, <u>seek those things which are above</u>, where Christ sitteth on the right hand of God. Set your affection on things above, <u>not on things on the earth</u>."

In other words, now that God has raised you up spiritually out of your sin and death and the whole system of evil (the world) that almost damned your soul to hell, don't go back into the world's system and seek the things that are in it — seek the things in the spiritual realm where Christ has seated you with Him!

Oh my, what an indictment upon 21st-century "Christianity"— especially in the United States! We've convinced ourselves that we have the ability to do both.

We convince ourselves that we love God and are passionate for Him, while we love money and are passionate for the things money can buy. We convince ourselves of our heart for the Lord, despite the fact that Jesus clearly said in Matthew 6:24,

> "No man can serve two masters: for either he will hate the one, and love the other; or else he will hold to the one, and despise the other. Ye cannot serve God and mammon."

Notice that Jesus said we CANNOT serve God and money! I mean, what terminology could He have used to make that point any stronger or any clearer? He didn't say we shouldn't; He said we *can't* do it. It's not possible. He didn't say that trying to live in two worlds in terms of the things we're passionate about is just a really hard thing to do. Jesus just flat out tells us, "You CANNOT do it! It is an IMPOSSIBILITY!"

We convince ourselves that we're where we need to be spiritually despite our passionate pursuit of the "things on the earth," even though the rest of God's commentary on that subject throughout the New Testament rings with the same clarity of Matthew 6:24 and Colossians 3:1-2!

I don't want to sound sarcastic, but I desperately want today's Christians to face the truth of the odd and very unbiblical brand of "Christianity" that is seemingly the norm in the 21st century. Because any way you slice the New Testament on this subject, I don't know that God could have been any more succinct or clear that we can't be passionate about the "things above" and at the same time be passionate about the "things on the earth." Let me mention just a few of these passages.

Chapter 3

How about Jesus' teaching in Matthew 6:19-20:

> "Lay not up for yourselves treasures upon earth, where moth and rust doth corrupt, and where thieves break through and steal: 20 But lay up for yourselves treasures in heaven, where neither moth nor rust doth corrupt, and where thieves do not break through nor steal:"

I mean, could He be any clearer? Don't lay up treasures <u>on earth</u>, but rather treasures <u>in heaven</u>! He contrasts the two! "Don't do this. But, do this!" And I can't even play dumb as if I don't really understand what "treasures on earth" are, because He spells it out for us! Treasures on earth are anything...

- Moths can eat (21st-century application — clothes)
- Rust can corrupt (21st-century application — cars)
- Thieves can break through (21st century application — cribs)[1]

I mean, do we really need someone to embellish the teaching of Matthew 6:19-20 for us to understand that?

And how about 1 John 2:15-16?

> "Love not the world, neither the things that are in the world. If any man love the world, the love of the Father is not in him. 16 For all that is in the world, the lust of the flesh, and the lust of the eyes, and the pride of life, is not of the Father, but is of the world."

Do you see what I'm talking about in terms of God's strength and clarity on this subject? Go back and read verse 15 again! How can we (myself included!) continue to make this world and the things that are in it our passionate pursuit and act like we don't know what God said that was an indication of?

We tend to justify ourselves with rationalizations like, "Well, I don't really LOVE money, the world, or the things in the world... I just LIKE them a lot!" Maybe we would say, "We're just FRIENDS. Yeah, that's it, FRIENDS." Sounds great, sounds like we made it through unharmed!

---

1 In other words, houses! But I like "cribs" better because it goes with "clothes" and "cars."

Until you read James 4:4...

> "...know ye not that the <u>friendship of the world</u> is <u>enmity with God</u>? whosoever therefore will be <u>a friend of the world is the enemy of God</u>."

Again, some pretty scathing stuff for most 21st-century Christians! And the truth is, I left off the most scathing part! Do you know what the lead-in is to this verse (James 4:4)? God says,

> "Ye <u>adulterers</u> and <u>adulteresses</u>, know ye not that the friendship of the world is enmity with God? whosoever therefore will be a friend of the world is the enemy of God."

Remember that when we were raised with Christ, we were placed in union with Him. The Spirit of God baptized us, or immersed us, into Christ's death, burial, and resurrection (1Co 12:13, Rom 6:3-5), and now we have become the bride of Christ. According to 2 Corinthians 11:2, we're now in the espousal (or engagement) period and are awaiting the consummation of our marriage to Christ. But when that day comes, Paul says Christ's intention is that we be presented to Him as a "chaste virgin." So we see that James is saying that after we've entered that relationship with Christ, if we try to maintain even a friendship with our old flame (the world), He views it as spiritual adultery!

My purpose in getting all of this out on the table isn't to guilt-trip you or in any way seek to put you under a "yoke of bondage" (Gal 5:1). My purpose is simply this: to allow God to take His word and reveal to us that we need a new passion for Him!

I want to end this chapter with a passage out of the Bible's great "Hall of Faith," Hebrews 11. This passage recounts some of the great Old Testament saints who actually "got it." I believe this passage is like reading God's commentary on His admonition to us in Colossians 3:1-2.

Read Colossians 3:1-2 again below, and see what connections you make to the passage in Hebrews 11:13-16 after it.

> Colossians 3:1 If ye then be risen with Christ, seek those things which are above, where Christ sitteth on the right hand of God. 2 Set your affection on things above, not on things on the earth.

Chapter 3

Hebrews 11:13 These all died in faith, not having received the promises, but having seen them afar off, and were persuaded of them, and embraced them, and confessed that they were strangers and pilgrims on the earth. 14 For they that say such things declare plainly that they seek a country. 15 And truly, if they had been mindful of that country from whence they came out, they might have had opportunity to have returned. 16 But now they desire a better country, that is, an heavenly: wherefore God is not ashamed to be called their God: for he hath prepared for them a city.

Meditate on these two passages until you see the connection.

Chapter 4
Passionately Pursuing God

In the last few chapters, we've been looking at the incredibly powerful work God did in saving us, what Colossians 3:1 calls being risen with Christ. To refresh your memory, here's Colossians 3:1-2 again:

> "If ye then be risen with Christ, seek those things which are above, where Christ sitteth on the right hand of God. 2 Set your affection on things above, not on things on the earth."

Let me identify a few key words in these verses that I think point us towards what God is trying to teach us.

First of all, the word *things*. *Things* are definitely the point at issue of these verses.

> "Seek those things which are above…"
> "Set your affection on things above, not on things on the earth."

Notice also two key verbs in these verses: the word *seek* and the word *set*.

The word *seek* carries with it the idea of what we are in pursuit of. He clearly commands us to seek, or to live our lives in pursuit of, the "things above." That's the affirmative (or positive) command. But just as clearly, and just as strongly, God commands us NOT to live our lives in pursuit of the "things on the earth." That's the negative command.

Now, we know what the "things on earth" are. We talked about those in the previous chapter: things moths can eat (clothes), things rust can corrupt (cars),

Chapter 4

and <u>things</u> thieves break through (cribs) so they can steal our other THINGS. Yeah, we know about the "things on earth," but what are those "things above"?

Whatever they are, we are to <u>set our affection</u> on those things. The word *affection* is sometimes translated elsewhere as "mind." But it's more than just our mind as we tend to understand it; it also includes our heart. That's why it is translated here as "affection." It's more than just what we THINK about — it also has to do with what we CARE about! The things we are PASSIONATE about!

God is saying in Colossians 3:1-2 that now that we have been spiritually raised from the dead with Christ (Col 2:12) and spiritually risen to sit with Him in heavenly places (Eph 2:6), there are some definite "things" we are to live our lives in passionate pursuit of, and there are some definite "things" we are to live our lives NOT in passionate pursuit of.

I believe with all of my heart that the key to keeping the flame of your passion burning for God the way that He wants it to burn (Rev 2:4-5) and the way YOU want it to burn toward Him (Eze 36:26-27) is in simply learning how to be obedient to these two verses.

Now, one thing is certain: We will never be able to live our lives <u>seeking</u> the things above and <u>setting</u> our affection on them unless we know WHAT we are to actually pursue and what it means to be passionate for those things!

To keep things digestible, we'll spend the next few chapters discussing the "things above" one at a time. Here's the first one.

Remember that salvation not only raised us out of the grave of our sin, it also raised us up to be seated in heaven ABOVE. Hey! That's where these things are that we're to be seeking! So, do this — connect with your spiritual self that is seated in heaven, allow your knowledge of the word of God to become a lens for you to look through, and tell me what you see.

I'm sure you see several things there, but isn't the first thing you see that "thing" that John identified in 1 John 5:7?

> "For there are three that bear record <u>in heaven</u>, the <u>Father</u>, the <u>Word</u>, and the <u>Holy Ghost</u>: and these three are one."

I assure you, as soon as we are raptured, the THING that will captivate us and consume us more than anything else in heaven is the first "thing above": the person of God.

I don't know how to say it any clearer than this: Now that we've been saved, God wants us to spend the remainder of our time on the earth SEEKING HIM! Earnestly seeking Him! Over and over through the word of God, God tells us to seek Him!

> Deuteronomy 4:29 says,
> "But if from thence thou shalt <u>seek</u> the LORD thy God, thou shalt <u>find</u> him, if thou <u>seek him with all thy heart and with all thy soul</u>."
>
> God said in Jeremiah 29:13,
> "And ye shall <u>seek</u> me, and <u>find</u> me, when ye shall <u>search</u> for me with <u>all your heart</u>."

That sounds a lot like having a passionate pursuit! Now, what is all of this about? Why is God continuously telling us in His word to seek Him? Is He lost? Is He hiding? Well, here's the way it shakes out biblically...

God created man to have an intimate, personal, love relationship with Him. As you probably know, through the tree God placed in the garden, God gave man a choice. God didn't create us as robots programmed only to love and pursue Him. God wanted us to love Him because we CHOSE to and because we WANTED to. And He wanted us to love Him not simply because of what He does, but because of who He is! And in the earliest days of creation, God would actually come down into the garden to walk in intimate fellowship with Adam in the cool of the day (Gen 3:8a).

Yet Adam made the fateful choice against God. Like Isaiah 53:6 says, he chose "his own way." He, along with his bride, chose to eat of the forbidden tree. And on that tragic day, God didn't come down into the garden the same way He had on each previous day. On this day, He came on a rescue mission. He came down into the garden with a question: "Adam, where art thou?" In other words, He came down to the earth seeking lost man. And the fact is, He's been seeking lost man ever since! In Luke 19:10, Jesus said,

> "For the Son of man is come to seek and to save that which was lost."

Chapter 4

If you know the Lord today, it's not because you just randomly found Him. You know Him today because He found you! You know Him because He went SEEKING you. Romans 3:11 says that our lostness was so absolutely devastating that it left us INCAPABLE of seeking Him!

"There is none that understandeth, there is none that <u>seeketh</u> after God."

But because He lovingly pursued after us, as He does for every person (Tit 2:11), we have now by faith entered the relationship with Him that we were created to have from the very beginning. And the point God is making in Colossians 3:1-2 when He tells us to seek Him is this: "Now that I've done all of this for you — because I went SEEKING for you when you were incapable of SEEKING ME, and because I LOVED you when you were incapable of LOVING Me (1Jo 4:10,19) — will you now SEEK ME? Will you passionately pursue that relationship with Me?"

Do you see what God is really after? It's what He's always wanted: for us to choose to love Him! That's what it means for us to seek Him and to set our affection on Him. That's why Jesus said that the greatest commandment is to love God with all of our HEART, and all of our SOUL, and all of our MIND, and all of our STRENGTH (Mark 12:30).

That's what God wants first and foremost and above everything else — for us to LOVE Him PASSIONATELY!

Do you know what is so sad? Most 21st-century Christians could say that they FEAR God. Most could say that they REVERE Him... that they SERVE Him... even OBEY Him. But how many could actually say that they LOVE Him? Do YOU love Him? Or have you left your "first love"? If you have, don't fret — go back to chapter one and revisit how to get back to that place you were when you first received salvation.

God is telling us in Colossians 3:1-2 that now that we are saved ("risen with Christ"), we are to SEEK the person of God and we are to SET our affection on Him because God wants us to be PASSIONATE about loving Him.

You say, "Well, how do I do that? How do I 'set my affection' (my mind and my heart) to loving Him?"

Well, check out the word *set*. When you're in your house or apartment and you begin to get a chill, what do you do? You go over and *set* the thermostat to the temperature you want it to be. You hear the furnace kick on, and suddenly the temperature rises to where it was *set*.

I challenge you to begin every day by SETTING the spiritual thermostat of your mind and heart through prayer to PASSIONATELY LOVE the person of God. See if it doesn't raise the temperature of your spiritual life to where you SET it!

To recap, the first "thing above" is the PERSON of GOD (1Jo 5:7). Why does God want us to SEEK HIM? Because He wants us to LOVE HIM PASSIONATELY (Mark 12:30)!

Take some time today to open your heart and talk to the Lord about your desire to passionately love Him with all of your heart.

Chapter 5

That I May Know Him

I've heard it noted that if the greatest commandment is to love God with all of our heart and soul and mind and strength (Mark 12:30), then the greatest sin is to NOT love God with all of our heart, soul, mind, and strength.

Wow! Which one of us can now say that we've never been guilty of committing a sin worse than murder, worse than adultery, worse than stealing, worse than… well, you name it! It's so easy for me to cruise along in my Christian life thinking I've got some things together, only to find that the reason I think I'm doing so well is that I don't really see my life the way God sees it. In the letter Jesus dictated to John to the church at Laodicea in Revelation 3:14-22, Jesus talked about our propensity to do just that, saying in Revelation 3:17…

> "Because thou <u>sayest</u>, I am rich, and increased with goods, and have need of nothing; and <u>knowest not</u> that thou art wretched, and miserable, and poor, and blind, and naked:"

Ouch! Isn't that a sobering rebuke and indictment upon those of us who think we've got it all together spiritually?

But rather than allowing the discovery of committing the greatest sin to depress us or put us under a truckload of self-condemnation and guilt, we should allow it to humble us before our God cause us to "groan within ourselves" (Rom 8:23) because of the great longing and passion within us to give God the glory that is due unto His name (Psa 29:2). That glory that we won't totally be able to express until we have experienced the fullness of our redemption, the redemption of our body (Rom 8:23). (And, just a little side note here: If you're not familiar with Romans 8:23 and the "groaning" Paul

Chapter 5

talked about in this verse, I'd suggest you take the time to familiarize yourself with the passage — Romans 8:18-23.)

Oh, where are the people in the 21st century who know the "groaning within ourselves" that Paul was talking about? I think Romans 8:23 sheds a whole different light on what it really means to seek and set our affection on the things above. I think we all have to ask ourselves, "Am I so passionately pursuing the things above that I groan within myself because of my longing for them?" God help us to search and to focus our hearts.

That last bit isn't directly related to our core content, but I didn't think we could really talk about what it's going to take to keep the fire of our passion for God burning intensely without a challenge to meditate on the "groaning" of Romans 8:23! But we're in the midst of trying to learn the truth God reveals in His Word that can keep us passionately loving the Lord Jesus Christ with a "first love" type of love (Rev 2:4), so let's get back to that.

We've landed right back in Colossians 3:1-2…

> "If ye then be risen with Christ, seek those things which are above, where Christ sitteth on the right hand of God. Set your affection on things above, not on things on the earth."

It's almost like God is saying to us, "Okay, now that you're saved, here's what I want you to do." How awesome is that? It's not Mark Trotter, your pastor, or any person for that matter, saying, "Now let me tell you what I think," or, "Let me share with you from my vast experience, blah, blah, blah." No, this is God saying, "Okay y'all, here's how this Christian life thing actually works!"

He tells us, "As you walk on earth, do it from the standpoint of where you are seated in heaven" (Eph 2:6, Col 3:1). In other words, "Live your life DOWN THERE passionately pursuing the things that are UP HERE!"

In the last chapter, we started identifying those "things" that we are to be seeking and what it means to set our affection on them. We saw that the very first thing above that we are to live our lives seeking is the PERSON of God (1Jo 5:7). We learned that setting our affection on Him means passionately LOVING HIM (Mark 12:30).

In this chapter, we'll look at the second thing that God reveals is above (in heaven) where we are seated with Him (Eph 2:6). Psalm 119:89 says,

"For ever, O LORD, thy word is settled in heaven."

That's the second thing that is above: the word of God. Look through your spiritual eyes — do you see it there? The holy, precious, infallible, unchanging, life-changing, incomparable, unconquerable, inexhaustible WORD of GOD! And God says, "Listen, now that you're saved, while you live out your life on the earth, I want you to live it passionately pursuing My word!"

Let's take a little space to identify the significance of the word of God in our lives and the point God is driving at in terms of our seeking it and setting our affection upon it. To do that, I want to look for a moment at the concept of God's name.

God repeatedly talks about His name. The name of God is a word that is used in reference to WHO He actually IS. It is the term God uses to refer to the completeness of His person — the sum total of all of His holy character and all of His glorious attributes. The concept is unbelievably powerful! And God has some very significant things to say about His name.

> Nehemiah 9:5 says...
> Blessed be thy glorious name, which is exalted above all blessing and praise.

In other words, anything you can find that is worthy of applause, a cheer, or a standing ovation, God's name dwarfs it!

> Philippians 2:9-11 says of Christ...
> Wherefore God also hath highly exalted him, and given him a name which is above every name: That at the name of Jesus every knee should bow...and that every tongue should confess that Jesus Christ is Lord, to the glory of God the Father.

Hallelujah to the NAME of Jesus! Hallelujah FOR the NAME of Jesus!

> Acts 4:12 says,
> Neither is there salvation in any other: for there is none other name under heaven given among men, whereby we must be saved.

Chapter 5

So, check it out...
His NAME is exalted above all blessing and praise...
His NAME is above every other name...
His NAME is the only one under heaven that has the power to save!

I mean, what more could you say about the name of God than that?! That's what makes these next verses in Psalm 138:1-2 so unbelievably powerful and far-reaching! David says...

> "I will praise thee with my whole heart: before the gods will I sing praise unto thee. I will worship toward thy holy temple, and praise thy name for thy lovingkindness and for thy truth: for thou hast magnified thy word above all thy name."

Say what? God magnified His word ABOVE His own NAME? How can these things be?

From a human standpoint, there is nothing that could ever be more blessed, more exalted, or more worthy of praise than the NAME of God. But! The only way that you could ever really KNOW His NAME... the only way you could ever even begin to comprehend that marvelous, infinite, matchless NAME... is through the WORD of GOD! That's how God has chosen to reveal Himself to us — through the pages of a supernatural Book! And without that Book, we would never be able to know Him! That, my friend, is what the psalmist is talking about here in Psalm 138:2! God magnified His Word ABOVE His own NAME because God is PASSIONATE about us KNOWING HIM!

In terms of Colossians 3:1-2, God is saying to us, "Now that you're saved, I want you to spend the rest of your life seeking my word! And I want you to daily set your affection upon it, because I want you to be PASSIONATE about KNOWING ME!"

This is why we study the word of God! Not to get information that can make us sound spiritual. Not so we can accumulate knowledge to promote ourselves, or to use as a weapon against others. Not so we can get rid of our guilt about not reading it. Not so we can tell everyone that we read through it in a year. Not so we can feel good about ourselves because we've read our prescribed number of chapters. No, no, no, and a thousand times NO!

God wants us to seek the truth of His Word for one reason: because we have a PASSION that burns inside of us to KNOW HIM! Isn't that the passion God Himself was trying to get us to understand in Jeremiah 9:23-24 when He said...

> "Thus saith the LORD, Let not the wise man glory in his wisdom, neither let the mighty man glory in his might, let not the rich man glory in his riches: But let him that glorieth glory in this, <u>that he understandeth and knoweth me</u>..."

And look at this promise of deliverance and blessing that God gives in Psalm 91:14! God says...

> "Because he hath <u>set</u> his <u>love</u> upon me, therefore will I deliver him: I will set him on high, <u>because he hath known my name</u>."

Setting our love? Does that sound familiar? This verse shows us so clearly that setting our love (our affection!) upon God is intertwined with knowing His name — the embodiment of His character — which we get to know through His word!

Do you see how important it is to God that we know Him? God wants it to be that important to us! He wants us to seek His word because He wants us to be passionate about knowing Him! He wants us to set our affection upon that!

Here's how this works practically:

God reveals to us through His word that the "things above" are those things that we are to be SEEKING while we live down here on the earth. And then, through prayer, we SET the spiritual thermostat of our hearts to those things. We cry out to God each day, and all through the day we pray something that might sound like this...

"Oh God, as I walk down here on the earth today, I want to live my life in the full reality of where You have seated me in heaven with You. And I want to seek those things that you allow me to see in this realm through the pages of Your word. I want to seek You today — Your PERSON. I joyfully and willfully SET the AFFECTION of my heart to LOVING YOU! I want to LOVE YOU today, with all of my heart, soul, mind, and strength!

Chapter 5

"I want to live my life today seeking Your WORD. Again, I joyfully and willfully SET the AFFECTION of my heart to KNOWING YOU! May it be the all-consuming, all-embracing, preoccupying passion of my very soul! As I go to Your word today, I pray with David, 'Open thou mine eyes, that I may behold wondrous things out of thy law' (Psalm 119:18). Things, Lord, that will help me to KNOW You more, because I believe the more I KNOW YOU, the more I will LOVE You! Oh, God, THAT is the passion of my heart. May my life reflect that passion today!"

This is what our risen life in Christ is all about (Col 3:1-2). This is what Christianity is all about! And I believe it is what God has revealed to us so we are able to maintain a constantly renewed passion for Him! May God help us today — and every other day — to keep this heavenly perspective.

Chapter 6

No Place of Departure

There have been some great men in the history of civilization. If Moses and Paul weren't the greatest, I think you'd have to agree that they certainly rank right up there! Man, how awesome would it be to have the opportunity to hang out with those ol' boys for an afternoon! Wouldn't that be a hoot? I know this: I'd be asking a lot of questions, and then I'd be keeping my fat trap shut!

And man, there are all kinds of things that we could talk about that contributed to their greatness, but there's one key thing that grabs me about these two men more than anything else. It wasn't their off-the-chart gifts, though they were both unbelievably gifted men. It wasn't their incredible IQ, though I would imagine that both of them were getting close to the "genius" numbers. It wasn't their great leadership abilities, it wasn't their organizational skills, though, again, all of these things and more were true about them!

The thing about these men that stands out to me more than anything else is the simple fact that with all that they had seen, heard, and experienced, they never came to a place of departure in their walk. Do you know what I'm talking about? I'm talking about that place of satisfaction that starts making us think we've arrived. That place of comfort which causes us to think that this is as good as it gets. That place where we are no longer hungering or thirsting for God. That place where we think we can put our spiritual lives on autopilot. That place where we think we'll be all right even though we no longer passionately pursue God.

I mean, think about my man Moses. He had a miraculous encounter with God at the burning bush. He saw God's flaming finger etch the Ten Commandments into tables of stone. He saw God's marvelous presence and power in

Chapter 6

the cloud by day and the pillar of fire by night as He lovingly guided the children of Israel on their journey. But despite all those wonderful, glorious, supernatural things, none of that was ever enough for Moses. None of that ever brought him to a place of spiritual complacence. He just kept going back up to the mountain! You hear the passion of his heart as he cries out to God in Exodus 33:18, "I beseech thee, shew me thy glory," or, how we might say it today, "I'm beggin' ya!"

And what about Paul? He was a guy who had at least three personal encounters with the risen and glorified Lord Jesus Christ. A man that was used by God to plant numerous churches throughout Asia Minor and Europe. A man used by God as the human author of half of the books in our New Testament. And yet, it wasn't enough. You hear him in Philippians 3:12-14 sharing the cry of his heart:

> "Not as though I had already attained, either were already perfect: but I follow after, if that I may apprehend that for which also I am apprehended of Christ Jesus. 13 Brethren, I count not myself to have apprehended: but this one thing I do, forgetting those things which are behind, and reaching forth unto those things which are before, 14 I press toward the mark for the prize of the high calling of God in Christ Jesus."

Did you catch the spirit in him that refused to find a place of departure? Did you catch the words he used in those verses? He says, "I don't think I've arrived… I follow after… I'm reaching forth… I press toward the mark." Imagine how intimately the great Apostle Paul actually knew the Lord Jesus Christ! And yet he passionately cries out in Philippians 3:10, "That I may know Him"!

Oh, how I hope that God will use this study to lead you and anyone else reading to embrace such a new passion for Him that for the rest of your life, you just constantly and passionately pursue Him! Constantly living in complete obedience to our calling in Colossians 3:1-2 and never again allowing there to be a place of departure in our spiritual walk!

Now, let's take a minute to talk about where we are in our study right now…

To help us to live our lives, as Paul said, constantly following after, reaching for, pressing toward, seeking the things above, and setting our affection upon them, we've tried to make sure that we understand just what "those things" actually are and what God actually intended by telling us to passionately pursue them.

We've looked at the first two already. I wonder if you could identify what they are, and what God is really seeking by telling us to seek them? Before you keep reading, see if you can.

The first "thing above" is the person of God, and God tells us to set our affection upon Him because God wants us to love Him.

The second "thing above" is the word of God, and God tells us to set our affection upon it because God wants us to know Him.

In this chapter, we'll look at the third "thing above" that God reveals to us through His word.

To see it, let me remind you that there are six men in the Bible who were beamed off of this planet straight up to the third heaven, the abode of God. One of those men got beamed up there and never came back down! His name was Enoch, a picture of the raptured church, and you can read about him in the great "Hall of Faith" in Hebrews 11:5. Another was Elijah, who was taken up to heaven in a whirlwind (2Ki 2:11). Another one was Paul, and in reference to the things he saw and heard, he said that God wouldn't allow him to utter a word about it! He talks about not being able to talk about it in 2 Corinthians 12:1-7.

But there were three other men who were caught up to the abode of God who WERE permitted to talk about it. What I think is interesting is that in all three accounts, they all mention one very specific thing that they saw: the throne of God. That's the third "thing above" the Bible reveals that we are to seek. Let's see what those other three men had to say about the throne of God.

Ezekiel talked about God's throne in Ezekiel 1:26-28, saying,

> "And above the firmament that was over their heads was the likeness of a THRONE, as the appearance of a sapphire stone: and upon the likeness of the THRONE was the likeness as the appearance of a man above upon it. 27 And I saw as the colour of amber, as the appearance of fire round about within it, from the appearance of his loins even upward, and from the appearance of his loins even downward, I saw as it were

Chapter 6

the appearance of fire, and it had brightness round about. 28 As the appearance of the bow that is in the cloud in the day of rain, so was the appearance of the brightness round about. This was the appearance of the likeness of the glory of the LORD. And when I saw it, I fell upon my face…"

Isaiah talked about the throne in Isaiah 6:1-3, saying,

"In the year that king Uzziah died I saw also the LORD sitting upon a THRONE, high and lifted up, and his train filled the temple. 2 Above it stood the seraphims: each one had six wings; with twain he covered his face, and with twain he covered his feet, and with twain he did fly. 3 And one cried unto another, and said, Holy, holy, holy, is the LORD of hosts: the whole earth is full of his glory."

The apostle John was the other one who saw the throne of God, and he wrote about it in Revelation 4:

"After this I looked, and, behold, a door was opened in heaven: and the first voice which I heard was as it were of a trumpet talking with me; which said, Come up hither, and I will shew thee things which must be hereafter. 2 And immediately I was in the spirit: and, behold, a throne was set in heaven, and one sat on the throne. 3 And he that sat was to look upon like a jasper and a sardine stone: and there was a rainbow round about the throne, in sight like unto an emerald. 4 And round about the throne were four and twenty seats: and upon the seats I saw four and twenty elders sitting, clothed in white raiment; and they had on their heads crowns of gold. 5 And out of the throne proceeded lightnings and thunderings and voices: and there were seven lamps of fire burning before the throne, which are the seven Spirits of God. 6 And before the throne there was a sea of glass like unto crystal: and in the midst of the throne, and round about the throne, were four beasts full of eyes before and behind. 7 And the first beast was like a lion, and the second beast like a calf, and the third beast had a face as a man, and the fourth beast was like a flying eagle. 8 And the four beasts had each of them six wings about him; and they were full of eyes within: and they rest not day and night, saying, Holy, holy, holy, Lord God Almighty, which was, and is, and is to come. 9 And when those beasts give glory and honour and thanks to him that sat on the throne, who liveth for ever and ever, 10 The four and twenty elders fall down before him that sat on the throne, and

> worship him that liveth for ever and ever, and cast their crowns before the throne, saying, 11 Thou art worthy, O Lord, to receive glory and honour and power: for thou hast created all things, and for thy pleasure they are and were created."

What a passage! In fact, it's a whole chapter dedicated to the throne room of God! If you were to open your Bible and underline each instance of the word "throne" in that chapter, do you know what you'd find? As John writes about what He saw in God's presence, 12 times in 11 verses he mentions the THRONE!

In each account, something significant is happening at that throne: WORSHIP. Passionate, life-changing WORSHIP! That's why God wants us to seek His THRONE above and set our affection there — He wants us to WORSHIP HIM!

In John 4:23, Jesus made it so clear that God is actually <u>seeking</u> our WORSHIP!

> "But the hour cometh, and now is, when the true worshippers shall worship the Father in spirit and in truth: for <u>the Father seeketh such to worship him.</u>"

I mean, what an absolutely mind-boggling thing that the God who is the Creator of all things is actually SEEKING our worship. I mean, I can't take it!

God doesn't seek our worship because He NEEDS it! No – not by 100 kazillion miles! And while we're at it, let's just go ahead and be perfectly clear about the fact that God not only doesn't NEED our WORSHIP, He NEEDS NOTHING! He doesn't need our money, our intellect, our ingenuity, our ideas, our opinions... or our anything else! If we don't worship Him, He remains just as holy, just as worthy, just as all-sufficient as He ever was! He doesn't NEED our worship. But man, does He WANT it! That's why He seeks it! Just stop and imagine this: God is up in heaven at this very second that you are reading these words, and He is seeking your worship! Unbelievable.

You'd think that something this unbelievable to us wouldn't be such a struggle — but it is, isn't it? Why is daily, passionate, true worship such a struggle? There is a life-changing answer!

Chapter 6

Ultimately, every single problem in the world can really be traced back to a battle over a THRONE and a struggle regarding WORSHIP. Sometime after the "beginning" in Genesis 1:1, Lucifer, the anointed cherub (Eze 28:14), desired the worship of which only God is worthy. He had a tremendously wicked thought that led to an unbelievably wicked plot. Isaiah 14:13-14 says that Lucifer said in his heart,

> "I will ascend into heaven, I will exalt my <u>throne</u> above the stars of God: I will sit also upon the mount of the congregation, in the sides of the north: 14 I will ascend above the heights of the clouds; <u>I will be like the most High</u>."

In Genesis 3 when the serpent sought to beguile the woman, Satan was "seeking" to come against the plan of God, beginning with destroying her ability to worship HIM! What has gone on in the world ever since that fateful day in the garden, what's behind all of Satan's lies and deception (Rev 12:9), and why he's seeking to devour us (1Pe 5:8), is that ultimately, he wants to devour our WORSHIP!

After we've been raptured and are casting ourselves at Christ's feet in true worship in heaven, down on the earth, the antichrist will come into the newly rebuilt temple in Jerusalem and take His seat on the (ahem!) THRONE and — you guessed it — demand to be WORSHIPPED!

All of history can be summarized as a battle over a throne! God is moving to put His Son there, and Satan is countering (and counterfeiting!) to get his sorry self there, and you and I find ourselves on a daily basis caught in the crossfire! God is on one side seeking our worship (John 4:23), and Satan is on the other side, seeking to counter that by seeking to devour us (1Pe 5:8).

And in the midst of the conflict, God comes along in Colossians 3:1-2 and gently tells us to seek the things above and set our affection on things above, not on things on the earth — not those things in Satan's domain! Satan is the "god of this world" (2Co 4:4). He's the "power" that is over the world's system from which we've been delivered (Eph 2:2). God says, "Don't go back into that domain and seek the things there!"

If God's throne is one of the things above and is the place of worship, then God is revealing to us that He wants us to daily set our affection (our mind and heart) to worship! He desires us to set the spiritual thermostat of our lives to passionate worship!

As we conclude this chapter, I want to take you back to those three men who were catapulted off of the earth to see the throne of God and the glory and the worship that surrounded it.

What happened at that throne was so utterly amazing and astounding that it brought the powerful prophet Ezekiel to a new sense of wonder and awe about the One seated upon it. He said in Ezekiel 1:28, "...and when I saw it, I fell upon my face."

For the great prophet Isaiah, what happened at that throne was so totally magnificent that it brought him to a whole new level of contrition, brokenness, and longing for personal holiness. He said in Isaiah 6:5, "Then said I, woe is me! for I am undone; because I am a man of unclean lips, and I dwell in the midst of a people of unclean lips: for mine eyes have seen the King, the LORD of hosts."

Lastly, what happened at that throne was so incredibly glorious that it brought the beloved Apostle John into a whole new dimension of love and adoration for the Lord Jesus Christ. It so arrested and amazed him that the one who laid his head on Jesus's chest during the last supper, when He saw Him in all of His glory, said in Revelation 1:17, "And when I saw him, I fell at his feet as dead."

God wants us to seek His THRONE because He wants us to see Him in the fullness of all that He really is. He wants us to see Him in the fullness of all of His glory. And He wants us to SET ourselves at that throne spiritually on a daily basis to WORSHIP HIM!

He wants it to be so amazing and astounding to us that, like Ezekiel, we're brought to a new sense of wonder and awe about the One on that throne every single day of our life.

He wants it to be so magnificent to us that, like Isaiah, we are brought to a new level of contrition and brokenness over sin and long in the depths of our soul for personal holiness on a daily basis. He wants it to be so glorious to us that, like John, we are brought into a new dimension of love and adoration for the Lord Jesus Christ where the most comfortable position is at His feet!

Chapter 6

Let's do what David talked about in Psalm 24:3 and "ascend into the hill of the Lord." I challenge you right now to ascend to His THRONE and WORSHIP HIM! Even with everything that is going on in this entire world, God in heaven is seeking your worship right now. May your worship of Him today be life-changing.

Chapter 7

Family in Heaven

The American brand of Christianity in this Laodicean church age knows little of the reality of the risen life that God was talking about in Colossians 3:1-2. (By "Laodicean," I'm referring to the seventh and final period of the history of the church just before the rapture, represented in the letter Jesus wrote in Revelation 3:14-22). And as I write about the subject of the risen life and the rarity of it in Christianity in the last days, I must confess… I am both. I am an American, and I am a Laodicean.

One of the characteristics Jesus said would be true of Christianity in the Laodicean period (the "perilous" last days to which Paul was referring in 2 Timothy 3:1-5) is that we think that we see the spiritual realm very clearly and don't realize that not only do we not see clearly, but we're actually BLIND, as Jesus says in Revelation 3:17! Gulp! He instructs us, then, to anoint our eyes with eyesalve that we may see (Rev 3:18). That's a great way to describe what the word of God is for those of us living in these last days: eyesalve to heal our blindness (Eph 1:17-18).

As an American and a Laodicean, I confess to you today that as I write about this incredible spiritual world described in Colossians 3:1-2 — that whole spiritual mindset that causes us to WALK on EARTH like someone SEATED in HEAVEN — I don't think for a minute that I totally see in that realm the full reality of what God is talking about. To be quite honest with you, in writing about it, I kind of feel like a guy enclosed in a high-fenced yard with a bunch of other people and we're unable to see beyond the fence, but I've found a little knot-hole. I've got my face pressed up against the Laodicean fence with my hands cupped around my temples, and I'm trying to describe what I'm seeing on the other side of the fence.

Chapter 7

All of that to say: I don't speak about the risen life from the standpoint of somebody hollering over to you from the other side of the fence. Man, I'm right there along with everybody else. But I do believe that if we'll keep anointing our eyes with the eyesalve of the word of God, that knot-hole will continue to get bigger and bigger, and ultimately it will be big enough for all of us to crawl out of and into the full realities of the spiritual life God intends on the other side.

Now, let's talk about where we are in terms of our study of Colossians 3. We've covered the first three things that the Bible reveals that are above and that we are to be passionately pursuing: the PERSON of GOD, the WORD of GOD, and the THRONE of GOD.

We have one more "thing above" that the Bible reveals to us. God reveals it to us in Ephesians 3:14-15. Paul is talking in this passage about how he was praying for the Ephesians. He says,

> "For this cause I bow my knees unto the Father of our Lord Jesus Christ, Of whom the whole <u>family in heaven</u> and earth is named."

That's the fourth thing that God reveals that is above and that is to be the passionate pursuit of our lives down here on the earth: the FAMILY of GOD. The question is, what does that mean? What does God have in mind when He says that we are to "seek" His family?

As we compare scripture with scripture (1Co 2:13), God reveals to us that seeking His family simply means that He wants us to MINISTER THROUGH HIM. Notice, not "FOR" Him, but "THROUGH" Him. Yes, there is a MINISTRY that He intends for you and me to be passionately involved in, but not in our own power and own strength — THROUGH His power, His filling, and His strength (2Co 3:4-5, Gal 2:20).

Our ministry through Him, as we "seek" the family of God, has two simple dimensions:

First of all, we are to MINISTER our GIFTS to those that are IN His FAMILY. That includes all of our brothers and sisters who are seated with us in heavenly places in Christ Jesus, and more specifically, all of our brothers and sisters who are seated with us in the same room on Sunday mornings!

The Bible teaches us that the moment we were saved, as the Spirit of God was raising us to new life in Christ, He was also bestowing upon us certain gifts that were given to us for the purpose of MINISTRY in our local Body of Christ (Rom 12:4-8, 1Co 12:12-31, Eph 4:7-16).

1 Peter 4:10 puts it this way:

> "As every man hath received the gift, even so minister the same one to another, as good stewards of the manifold grace of God."

I ask you to search your heart today. Are you seeking the family of God? That is, are you actively and passionately seeking to minister to your brothers and sisters through Christ's power in the ministry of your local church? It's not just what your pastor would want, though I'm sure he would! God Himself reveals that that's what HE wants of our lives now that we're risen with Him! But not only does seeking to minister through Him involve ministering our gifts to those who are in His family; it also means that we are to minister the GOSPEL to those He INTENDS to be in His family!

God wants to use YOU to see other worshippers take their seat with the rest of His family in heaven! He wants that to be what we're seeking as we walk down here on the earth. He wants us to be passionately pursuing those who are outside of His family with the gospel of Jesus Christ! He so wants us living in the reality of where we're seated with His glorious family in heaven (Eph 3:15) that we see the people down on the earth that we work with, go to school with, are friends with, are neighbors with, are related to, as people our loving Father wants to be in His family!

That's the risen life that God is talking about in Colossians 3:1-2. A life that is all about the passionate pursuit of LOVING Him, KNOWING Him, WORSHIPPING Him, and MINISTERING through Him. I challenge you to set your affection on "those things." And, as a child of God who loves Him, knows Him, and worships Him, pray that God would give you the glorious privilege of MINISTERING through Him today — to minister your gifts to those who are in His family and to minister the gospel to those He intends to be in His family.

Chapter 8

The Wrong Passions

As we started our journey down the Colossians 3 path, I called your attention to two key verbs in verses 1 and 2: the word *seek* and the word *set*. Through those two verses, I believe that in a practical sense, God is telling us that now that we're saved ("risen with Christ" – 3:1), if we will keep ourselves passionate about Him, and if we will constantly live our lives with a "first love" (Rev 2:4) type of passion, we must, first of all…

1. TALK TO GOD DAILY ABOUT THE PURSUITS AND PURPOSES OF LIFE. (Col 3:1-2)

Namely, through prayer…

To seek the PERSON of GOD, because God wants us to LOVE HIM.
To seek the WORD of GOD, because God wants us to KNOW HIM.
To seek the THRONE of GOD, because God wants us to WORSHIP HIM.
To seek the FAMILY of GOD, because God wants us to MINISTER through HIM.

I don't think I can over-emphasize the importance of coming before God at the beginning of each day and, through prayer, allowing Him to bring us into a conscious awareness of what it is that He wants us to be seeking. And I don't think I can over-emphasize the importance of, again, through prayer, setting the spiritual thermostat of our heart each morning to fulfill God's desires and purposes for our new life in Him. I have found that without allowing God to take me into the spiritual locker room and remind me of His game plan, the chances of me living in the reality of where I'm spiritually seated and the chances of me actually loving, knowing, worshipping, and ministering

Chapter 8

through Him are somewhere between slim and none. We ought to bring to the Lord those earthly pursuits which seek to consume us and ask for Him to help us maintain focus on the things above.

Listen, what we're learning together from Colossians 3:1-2 can't just be something we're seeking to apply to our lives at church, on a missions trip, with our family, or in any other individual piece of our lives. What we're talking about here is Christianity 101! God is showing us in this passage, "This is My basic game plan for your life now that you're saved!" These aren't things we do to become "super saints" or to have the deeper Christian life! These are just the basic components for spiritual "survival" — this is just the normal Christian life!

If we will constantly live with the passion for God that He so wants us to have, there is another key verb that must also become a part of our daily practice. It is the word *mortify* in verse 5.

God tells us in verses 5-7 that now that we're saved...

> "Mortify therefore your members which are upon the earth; fornication, uncleanness, inordinate affection, evil concupiscence, and covetousness, which is idolatry: 6 For which things' sake the wrath of God cometh on the children of disobedience: 7 In the which ye also walked some time, when ye lived in them."

In a very practical sense, I think the point is this...

2. TALK TO GOD DAILY ABOUT THE PASSIONS OF OUR BODY.

Oh, this is so important! Here's the deal…

As we have learned together from Colossians 2:12, our salvation meant that we DIED with Christ, we were BURIED with Him, and — since the same resurrection power that God put into operation when He raised Christ from the dead was put into operation in us when we expressed faith in Him — we were RISEN with Christ. And what a transformation that was! In 2 Corinthians 5:17, it says,

> "Therefore if any man be in Christ, he is a new creature: old things are

The Wrong Passions

passed away; behold, all things are become new."

Listen to that! "All things are become new!" And He's referring to the newness in our soul and spirit. Hallelujah! But the fact is, the transformation that took place in our soul and spirit when we were redeemed is still housed in the same physical body we had before we were placed in Christ. Ephesians 1:12-14 says we're still awaiting "the redemption of the purchased possession."

In Romans 8:23, Paul sheds light on what he was actually referring to when he talked about the "redemption of the purchased possession." He says...

"...even we ourselves groan within ourselves, waiting for the adoption, to wit, the <u>redemption of our body</u>."

Yes, when we were saved, Christ purchased us — every part of us: spirit, soul and body (1Co 6:20, 1Th 5:23). And at salvation, our spirit and soul experienced its glorious redemption; however, the redemption of our body is something that we will not actually "inherit" (Eph 1:14, 1Co 15:50-57) until the rapture, at which time Paul says in Philippians 3:20-21...

"The Lord Jesus Christ...shall change our vile body, that it may be fashioned like unto his <u>glorious body</u>."

The point is, we don't have that glorified body yet! That's why Paul says in Colossians 3:3-5...

"For ye are dead, and your life is hid with Christ in God. 4 When Christ, who is our life, shall appear, then shall ye also appear with him in glory. 5 <u>Mortify therefore your members which are upon the earth</u>..."

I want you to notice that word *therefore*. It's such a key to understanding these verses! You see, verse 3 is reiterating the point of Colossians 2:12 — that our salvation meant we died with Christ, are risen with Him, and our whole life is all about Him now because we are IN HIM. And Paul says in verse 4 that when Christ appears, that's when we'll experience the "redemption of our body" (Rom 8:23) and receive that "glorified body" like Christ's (Php 3:21). But Paul is saying that since we don't have that glorified body yet, we must <u>therefore</u> mortify the one we have! And he tells us here that the reason it must be dealt with is because this unredeemed body has all kinds of sinful, sexual passions that are lodged in the very fabric of it. And those passions, Paul says,

Chapter 8

must be MORTIFIED — they must be put to DEATH!

Do you remember me telling you that Colossians and Ephesians are twin epistles? That they cover the same basic ground, but from just enough of a different slant that they shed light on each other? Well, Ephesians 2:3 talks about how in our lost state, we lived our lives "fulfilling the desires of the flesh." In Colossians 3:5, God tells us exactly what the "desires of the flesh" actually revolve around — namely, sex. And I don't think we need any commentary to understand that.

But in Colossians 3:5, Paul gives us great insight into the whole path that leads to sexual sin. He takes us in verse 5 from the FRUIT of sexual sin (FORNICATION, the "act" with which it ends) back to the ROOT of sexual sin (COVETOUSNESS, the "attitude" with which it begins). Follow the progression...

He says that sexual sin actually begins with the sin of covetousness, which he identifies as IDOLATRY. Wow! Check that out! Covetousness isn't just "like" idolatry — it IS idolatry! And covetousness is very simply the sin of wanting more. Wanting more than what God wants me to have, or wanting more than God wants me to have NOW. It could be money, it could be circumstances, or it could be in the sexual realm. But all covetousness begins with a desire for something God says is "out of bounds." (For singles, sex before marriage. For married folks, sex outside of marriage). And God says to MORTIFY that desire... that covetousness... that IDOLATRY!

But, if we don't mortify our covetousness, it leads to the next thing: evil concupiscence. *Concupiscence* is a big, hairy word that has to do with those lustful desires that clang around in these bodies. And God calls them EVIL.

So, once I say "yes" to my flesh and allow myself to desire more than God wants me to have (covetousness), it begins a furnace burning on the inside of me, creating a heightened barrage of evil desires in my flesh (evil concupiscence). This leads to the next thing: inordinate affection. Inordinate affection is very closely related to evil concupiscence, but it's another step down the road. The fire inside is burning hotter. The evil desires are further heightened. The MIND begins to think about ways to actually fulfill those desires.

Then, those passions begin to manifest themselves in the next thing: uncleanness. The flesh begins to act on its sinful lusts, passions, and desires, which then leads, of course, to the actual act of fornication. And God is so strong when He talks to us about fornication!

In Acts 15:29, He says ABSTAIN from it!
In Acts 21:25, He says KEEP from it!
In 1 Corinthians 6:18, He says FLEE from it!
In 1 Corinthians 7:2, He says AVOID it!
In 1 Corinthians 10:8, He says don't COMMIT it!
In Ephesians 5:3, He says don't let it ONCE BE NAMED AMONG YOU.
And in Colossians 3:5, He says KILL IT! MORTIFY IT!

He tells us in verses 6 and 7 that living according to the passions of our body is what He saved us out of! He reminds us that living life according to the sinful passions of our bodies is the very reason His wrath falls (and will fall) upon the children of DISOBEDIENCE. And the point is, that's not us anymore! We're the children of OBEDIENCE! We're the children of God! Through our death, burial, and resurrection with Christ, He raised us out of that whole sexual world. It has absolutely no place with who we are in Christ, and certainly no place with where we are seated with Him! So He says, "Yes, I know you don't have a redeemed, glorified body yet! So MORTIFY the one you have!"

But the question is, how do we MORTIFY those passions and desires? I know of no other way than simply talking with Him very specifically in prayer about the passions of our body that He details for us in verse 5. Through prayer, we can present our bodies "a living sacrifice, holy, acceptable unto God," which is our reasonable service (Rom 12:1).

Through prayer, we can yield our members (the members of our bodies) not as instruments of unrighteousness into sin, but yield ourselves to God, "as those that are alive from the dead" (i.e. risen with Christ, Col 3:1), and our members as "instruments of righteousness unto God" (Rom 6:13).

Through prayer, we can acknowledge the full reality of what Paul talked about in Galatians 5:24:

> "And they that are Christ's have crucified [i.e. MORTIFIED, Col 3:5] the flesh with the <u>affections</u> and <u>lusts</u>."

My, oh my, what a practical book the Bible is! The Bible has everything we

Chapter 8

need for life on this earth to be as abundant as Jesus talked about (John 10:10). We just need to BELIEVE it and APPLY it!

Let's apply it right now: today, talk to God about the PURSUITS and PURPOSES of LIFE (Col 3:1-4) and about the PASSIONS of your BODY (Col 3:5-7).

Chapter 9
The Simple Life

That's right! The Christian life really is very simple (2Co 11:3). But please make sure you don't confuse SIMPLE with EASY, because it's anything BUT easy! In fact, not only is it hard — it's impossible! That's why the whole message of the New Testament is that our calling as believers isn't about us living FOR Christ, but Christ living THROUGH us (Php 3:9, Col 2:6, Rom 3:20-22, Gal 2:20, 2Co 4:8-10). That's how you live the Christian life — not by TRYING… but by DYING! We have to get out of the way so that Christ can live THROUGH us!

That's what makes the things we've been looking at from Colossians 3 so important. Because God is very practically walking us through His plan for how the fullness of Christ can be lived out IN and THROUGH us. The passage is teaching us…

1. Talk to God daily about the pursuits and purposes of life (3:1-4)
2. Talk to God daily about the passions of the body (3:5-7), and now, a third thing…

3. TALK TO GOD DAILY ABOUT THE PERIL OF SELF (3:8-9)

God tells us in verses 8-9…

> "But now ye also <u>put off</u> all these; anger, wrath, malice, blasphemy, filthy communication out of your mouth. 9 Lie not one to another, seeing that ye have <u>put off</u> the old man with his deeds;"

He tells us we are to PUT OFF the OLD MAN — the old YOU, your old SELF.

Chapter 9

You see, before we experienced our death, burial, and resurrection with Christ (Col 2:12, 3:1a), SELF sat on the throne in our lives. SELF called the shots. And SELF wanted what SELF wanted — and, buddy, when SELF didn't get SELF'S way, it ticked SELF off! It made us angry. Now, put the brakes on for just a second.

Do you remember how in the last chapter, we saw God talking about the whole process that takes place in the sexual realm of the "fulfilling of the desires of the flesh" (Eph 2:3)? He listed the sins of the flesh, working from the FRUIT of sexual sin back to the ROOT of it.

Well, in Colossians 3:8-9, He's detailing for us "the desires of the mind" that He talked about in Ephesians 2:3. He's detailing for us that whole way of thinking that we used to have when SELF was seated on the throne of our life. And He gives us the progression of how the sins of the mind actually find their expression. This time, however, He begins with the ROOT (the attitude): anger. Then, He works us to the FRUIT (the action): lying.

And God says it goes like this...

When I'm living according to the OLD me, SELF wants its own selfish way. And when I don't get my way, an attitude rises up in my mind: anger. And unless I PUT IT OFF, the attitude of anger in me moves into the explosion of wrath. Then comes malice: wrath that won't let up and is now seething. And then malice gives way to blasphemy. Now usually when we think of blasphemy, we think of someone profaning the name of the Lord. Paul lets us know here, however, that when we allow the buildup of our frustrated self-will to spew out venom against another person, we are guilty of the sin of blasphemy!

That blasphemy leads to the next thing: filthy communication out of our mouth. Oh my, the words that can come out of people's mouths (even Christians!) when they allow themselves to be escalated into a fit of rage! And then, filthy communication out of our mouth leads to the next thing: lying.

What happens is that we allow ourselves to get so totally cheesed off that all our ranting and raving has now pushed whatever it was that got under our skin in the first place into something it never was. We like to call it exaggerating — God calls it LYING.

And He says to us, "Listen. Now that you've been RISEN WITH CHRIST, totally do away with that old SELF LIFE you used to live when SELF sat on the throne! PUT OFF anything and everything that has to do with that life!"

It's time that we stop rationalizing and justifying ourselves with lame excuses like, "Well, I've just always had a bad temper," or, "I'm just like my Dad," or, "It's this red hair," or, "I'm Irish." God doesn't give room for excuses. He says to PUT OFF all of that junk!

But how do we actually PUT OFF those things He lists in verses 8 and 9? We do it through prayer. So talk to God daily about the peril of self.

Then, God shows us a fourth thing in terms of keeping our hearts passionate for Him and allowing His life to be lived through us...

4. TALK TO GOD DAILY ABOUT THE PRIORITIES OF CHRIST (3:10-16)

Yes, we certainly must PUT OFF THE OLD MAN. But the admonition doesn't stop there! So many people keep trying and trying to overcome their tendency to fly off the handle, but it never seems to work for them. The reason is very simple. You will never keep the old man OFF without PUTTING ON THE NEW MAN! The first key verb in this section is PUT ON. Paul tells us in verses 10-14...

> "And [ye] have PUT ON the new man, which is renewed in knowledge after the image of him that created him: 11 Where there is neither Greek nor Jew, circumcision nor uncircumcision, Barbarian, Scythian, bond nor free: but Christ is all, and in all. 12 <u>Put on</u> therefore, as the elect of God, holy and beloved, bowels of mercies, kindness, humbleness of mind, meekness, longsuffering; 13 Forbearing one another, and forgiving one another, if any man have a quarrel against any: even as Christ forgave you, so also do ye. 14 And above all these things <u>put on</u> charity, which is the bond of perfectness."

Notice several things. First of all, that the NEW MAN is renewed in knowledge (v. 10). Obviously, he's referring to the knowledge of the word of Christ (v. 16).

Chapter 9

Secondly, notice that the eight things he specifically tells us to PUT ON in verses 12 through 14 are all things that Christ PUT ON so that we could be made new creatures (2Co 5:17)... or a NEW MAN (Col 3:10). These eight things are actually what brought Christ to the cross when He died our death. It was His bowels of mercies, kindness, humbleness of mind, meekness, long-suffering, forbearance, forgiveness, and above all these things, charity, which is the bond of perfectness. And God says, "Listen, now that you've been RISEN WITH CHRIST, in all of your dealings with people — and especially when people violate you — you just PUT ON everything Christ PUT ON when He responded to how you had violated Him!" My oh my, don't miss applying those things God lists in verses 12-14! The Christian life doesn't get any more BASIC or DEEP than that!

And then, notice the next key verb in this section concerning Christ's priorities for our lives. Verse 15 says,

> "And <u>let</u> the peace of God rule in your hearts, to the which also ye are called in one body; and be ye thankful."

You see, back in Colossians 1:20, He already taught us that Christ "made peace through the blood of his cross," and through it, reconciled us to Himself. We are now under the rule of Christ, and therefore under the rule of peace. God simply tells us in verse 15 to LET it rule in our hearts. Oh, listen to that word! So many believers allow themselves to be ruled by something other than peace. They're ruled by fear, worry, anxiety, anger, bitterness, lust, people, and all kinds of other things that have nothing whatsoever to do with our calling in Christ. You can always tell the people who let the peace of God rule in their hearts because PEACEFUL people are THANKFUL people. That peace they have in their heart produces an attitude of gratitude toward God and toward others.

And then there's one other key verb in this section, which happens to be the word LET once again. You see it in verse 16...

> "<u>Let</u> the word of Christ dwell in you richly in all wisdom; teaching and admonishing one another in psalms and hymns and spiritual songs, singing with grace in your hearts to the Lord."

Notice it's not just a matter of memorizing the word of Christ. That's a great start! But Paul tells us here that we must LET it DWELL in us richly in all wisdom. In other words, it can't just be in our memory banks! It must find a "settled place" (1Ki 8:13) in every part of the fabric of our entire being so that we're living our lives not according to the "desires of the flesh and of the mind" (Eph 2:3), but according to the desires of Christ as they are revealed in the truth of His word. From this, we learn we ought to TALK TO GOD DAILY ABOUT THE PRIORITIES OF CHRIST.

Which really leads to the fifth thing...

5. TALK TO GOD DAILY ABOUT THE PRESENCE OF CHRIST (3:17)

Verse 17 is like the conclusion to the risen life. Paul says...

> "And whatsoever ye do in word or deed, do all in the name of the Lord Jesus, giving thanks to God and the Father by him."

Now God began this entire passage saying, "Okay, now that you're saved, here's the game plan I want you to follow..." And from there, He lays out seven key verbs...

- SEEK the things above
- SET your affection on things above, not on things on the earth
- MORTIFY your members
- PUT OFF the old man
- PUT ON the new man
- LET the peace of God rule in your heart
- LET the word of Christ dwell in you richly in all wisdom

And when all of these things are happening, verse 17 says that every word we speak with our mouth should be spoken "in the name of the Lord Jesus" and every deed we do should be done "in the name of the Lord Jesus." This means that before we open our mouth to speak, we ought to be able to preface it by saying, "Now, what I'm about to say, I'm going to say because I believe that if Christ were here, this is what He would say! So, I'm going to speak this in His name, or, 'on His behalf.'" And it means that before we do anything with or through our body, we ought to be able to preface that action by saying,

Chapter 9

"Now, what I'm about to do, I'm going to do because I believe that if Christ were here, this is what He would do! So, I'm going to do this deed in His name, or 'on His behalf.'"

What if that rule of thumb (or rather, rule of Christ!) permeated our lives at home, at work, with the lost people in our circle of influence, with the people in our church body? Can you imagine how that might change the things we say to and about people? Can you imagine how that might change the things we do with these bodies? Now, I'm certainly not suggesting that we actually preface our words and our deeds with these words — I'm simply saying, we ought to be able to!

Let me close this chapter with an outline of the first 17 verses of Colossians 3. Make sure you have these things in your mind and in your heart.

1. TALK TO GOD DAILY ABOUT THE PURSUITS AND PURPOSES OF LIFE (3:1-4)
- SEEK the things above
- SET your affection on things above, not on things on the earth

2. TALK TO GOD DAILY ABOUT THE PASSIONS OF THE BODY (3:5-7)
- MORTIFY your members

3. TALK TO GOD DAILY ABOUT THE PERIL OF SELF (3:8-9)
- PUT OFF the old man

4. TALK TO GOD DAILY ABOUT THE PRIORITIES OF CHRIST (3:10-16)
- PUT ON the new man
- LET the peace of God rule in your heart
- LET the word of Christ dwell in you richly in all wisdom

5. TALK TO GOD DAILY ABOUT THE PRESENCE OF CHRIST (3:17)
- Every WORD spoken in Jesus's name
- Every DEED done in Jesus's name

If you've ever struggled with how to pray or what to talk to God about when you pray, Colossians 3:1-17 is the best prayer list I've ever seen! I hope we'll all allow this passage to become a daily part of our lives. Oh my, what our LIVES could be if we would... what our HOMES could be if we would... what our CHURCHES could be if we would!

Chapter 10

A Fly on the Prison Wall

One of the passages of Scripture that has always intrigued me is the account of Jesus praying in Luke 11:1-2. I mean, wouldn't you have loved to have been a fly on the wall to hear the intimacy and the passion of His heart as He prayed? Not to mention the actual content of His prayer!

Well, whatever was happening as Jesus prayed in Luke 11, by the time He had finished, it was enough to let His disciples know that they didn't really know a whole lot about prayer! Luke 11:1 says that in response to listening to Jesus pray…

> "One of his disciples said unto him, Lord, teach us to pray, as John also taught his disciples."

And you know what's so intriguing about that to me? The disciples had heard Jesus preach some incredible sermons, but they never said, "Lord, teach us to preach like that!" They had witnessed Him perform unbelievable miracles, but they never said, "Lord, teach us to do miracles like that!"

But, check it out… they heard Him pray, and they just had to ask Him, "Lord, would you teach us to pray like that?" Listen, for that to have been their response, the intimacy and passion of His voice must have gripped them in their soul. The content of His prayer must have just totally blown them away! It makes me want to say with them, "Lord, teach me to pray!"

And what got me thinking about that is the passage we've been using to guide us throughout this book, Colossians 3:1-17. In my estimation, I believe it could be called the manifesto of the Christian life. It's God peeling off some

Chapter 10

space to say, "Okay, now that you're saved, let me take 17 simple verses to teach you how to keep your heart both tender and passionate toward Me. Let Me teach you the nuts and bolts of how the Christian life works and how it all fits together. If you get this, it will impact every area of your life, beginning with the two biggest areas: your FAMILY (Col 3:18-21) and your JOB (Col 3:22-4:1)."

And I can't help but wonder what Paul must have thought after he had penned the first 17 verses of Colossians 3. I believe after receiving these incredible words inspired by the very Spirit of God Himself, Paul's prayer life had to have taken on a whole different flavor. I think Paul would have understood that the only way to actually be obedient to the seven key verbs the Spirit of God wrapped this passage around is through PRAYER. I mean, for real now, how else could you possibly...

- SEEK the things above
- SET your affection on things above
- MORTIFY your members
- PUT OFF the old man
- PUT ON the new man
- LET the peace of God rule in your heart
- LET the word of Christ dwell in you richly in all wisdom

Again, the only activity I can think of that would allow us to actually put these commands into practice is prayer! And oh my, wouldn't you have loved to be that fly on the wall (and in Paul's case, most of the time, it would have been a prison wall!) to hear Paul actually pray through this incredible passage the Spirit of God had inspired him to write? If he were around today, I wonder if it wouldn't sound something like this...

"Oh Lord, what an awesome God You are! Your grace, Your mercy, Your love, and Your power is nothing but amazing! There's no other word I know to use, no other word seems to fit, and even 'amazing' doesn't capture the full essence of how my heart wants to communicate it. I guess I'm trying to say that You're just indescribable! I praise You, God, for who You are! There is no one and no thing that compares with You. You alone are God, and there are no runners-up!

"But, not only do I praise You for who You are, I praise You for all You've done! When I think about Your death and burial, and then the incredible power of resurrection, it's more than my heart can take. And then, when I come to grips with the fact that when I called upon your name, the Spirit of God actually placed me into Your death, and I died with You... placed me into Your burial, and I was buried with You... and then, placed me into Your resurrection, and I was raised from the dead with you spiritually, by the same exact power that raised You from the dead physically (Col 2:12, Rom 6:3-5). Oh my, not only is it more than my HEART can take, it's hard for my MIND to take. I find it hard to fully comprehend the incredible power You exercised in saving me, not to mention the incredible power that now resides in me (Acts 1:8). Oh, Father, I want to live my life today in the fullness of that power (Php 3:10). I willfully yield myself to the power of Your Spirit within me (Rom 6:13). I surrender all that I am to Your Lordship. I pour myself out to You, longing for the complete filling of Your Spirit and the full release of the Spirit's power in and through me today (Col 2:6, Gal 5:16, 22-25).

"And, oh God, I recognize that the resurrection power that raised me out of the death of my sins also raised me to sit with You in heavenly places (Eph 2:6). Oh, how I want to live my life down here on the earth in the full reality of where I'm seated with You spiritually (Col 3:1). As I go through my day today, may I be totally unplugged from the world's system of evil all around me (Gal 1:4) — that system of evil that Satan sought to use to hold me captive at his will before You reached down and delivered me (2Ti 2:26). Oh, may I not go back and seek the things in that system! May I totally be plugged into those things which are above in this heavenly kingdom where I'm seated with You today (Col 3:2).

"As I look through the eyes of faith and through the lens of Your Word, I see You today, Lord, in the fullness of Your glorious PERSON (1Jo 5:7). Oh, may I seek You today with all of my heart, soul, mind, and strength (Deu 4:29, Jer 29:13) and in so doing, may I offer You what it is that You're seeking. May I LOVE You today with all of my heart, soul, mind and strength (Mark 12:30). I set my affection towards LOVING You today; I SET the spiritual thermostat of my heart towards You.

"And oh Lord, as I look at where I'm seated with You today, I see Your glorious WORD (Psa 119:89). And oh, may I seek IT today! I set my affection on it, knowing that it is how You have chosen to reveal Yourself to me (Psa 138:2). Oh God, with everything that is within me, I long to KNOW You

Chapter 10

(Php 3:10). I don't go to Your Word today out of a sense of obligation or duty; I go because of the passion in my heart to know You (Psa 27:8). I cry out with David, "Open thou mine eyes, that I may behold wondrous things out of thy law" (Psa 119:18). Help me to KNOW You more today.

"I see You today, through the eyes of faith, seated upon Your glorious THRONE (Eze 1:26-28, Isa 6:1-3, Rev 4:1-11). Oh, how wonderful You are (Isa 9:6)! It's almost as if I can hear the angels as they lift their voices to praise You, the triune God, crying Holy! Holy! Holy! I join them today; I join the WORSHIP in heaven today. With my lips I declare Your greatness and Your glory (Heb 13:15). But oh God, I realize today that what comes out of my LIPS only has credence if it is backed up by my life (Isa 1:10-20). So, oh Lord, may my whole life be an expression of WORSHIP to You today. May I be what You've called me to be — a TRUE WORSHIPPER (John 4:23). Through my LIFE and my LIPS today, receive WORSHIP... TRUE WORSHIP! May it passionately flow through my spirit, and from there into my heart, my soul, and my mind, so that like David, I may bless you, Lord, with "all that is within me" (Psa 103:1). May my worship be prompted today by Your Truth, for "thy word is truth" (John 17:17). May the truth of Your Word both generate and regulate my worship today. May Your preeminence and the worship for which I count You worthy be seen by the place of preeminence I give to the word of truth today (Psa 119:133).

"And oh God, as I look around me through the eyes of faith and of scripture, I see your FAMILY (Eph 3:14-15) already seated here spiritually in Your presence (Eph 2:6). Oh God, You are not just our God, and we are not just Your people (2Co 6:16). You are also our Father, and we are Your sons and daughters (2Co 6:18)! Oh, how You love Your FAMILY (1Jo 3:1)! And because of Your love for the FAMILY, help me today to love Your FAMILY as well (John 13:34, 1Jo 4:11). Help me to seek Your FAMILY! May I take the gifts You have graciously blessed me with and entrusted to me and through the power of Your Spirit in me, MINISTER those gifts to those who are IN Your FAMILY (1Pe 4:10). Use me, today, Lord!

"And Father, as I behold this FAMILY seated here today, I know that You are not willing that any should perish, but that all should come to repentance (2Pe 3:9). I know that it is Your desire that the whole world be born into Your FAMILY (John 3:16)! And today, may my affection — my mind and my heart — be SET on allowing You to also MINISTER THROUGH ME the GOSPEL to all of those around me that you INTEND to be in Your

FAMILY (Acts 20:24). I pray specifically that You will open doors of utterance to me today (Col 4:3) so that I can tell others that the God of creation died, was buried, and rose again for them and now wants to live in them (Col 1:27)! Use me to see someone born into Your FAMILY today (John 3:3)!

"Lord, I know that these are the things that the RISEN LIFE of the Lord Jesus in me is passionately pursuing today (Eze 36:26-27). But while His Spirit in me is soaring toward those 'things above,' Lord, I recognize that I'm still living down here on earth, in a body made of flesh, that has not yet experienced its redemption (Eph 1:14, Rom 8:23). Sometimes, Lord, I feel like my body is this big old chunk of metal and this world's system of evil (Gal 1:4) with the lust of the flesh, the lust of eyes, the pride of life (1Jo 2:16) like a huge magnet seeking to pull me down and keep me living in the earthly realm. Oh God, demagnetize me today! Through Your Spirit (Rom 8:13) and Your Word (Col 3:16), MORTIFY this body of flesh that I live in today. May all of its passions be PUT TO DEATH because of the PASSION that I have in my heart for You (1Pe 1:13-16). Help me not to live my life in that whole world of 'fornication, uncleanness, inordinate affection, evil concupiscence, and covetousness, which is idolatry' (Col 3:5). I know those things were characteristic of my life prior to knowing You, and that they are characteristics now in the lives of people who don't know You (Col 3:6-7) — but Lord, I do know You! So today, I present my body to you a living sacrifice (Rom 12:1). I yield to You the members of my body as instruments of righteousness (Rom 6:13). I groan within myself today, awaiting the redemption of this body (Rom 8:23) — that time when it is glorified, like Yours (Php 3:21, Col 3:4)! But until then, may the affections and lusts of my body be crucified with You (Gal 5:24, 2:20).

"And Lord, along with MORTIFYING the desires of my flesh (Eph 2:3a, Col 3:5), I willfully seek to PUT OFF the desires of my mind (Eph 2:3b). I willfully seek to PUT OFF THE OLD MAN — that old way of thinking that I had back when the old me, my old self, used to sit on the throne of my life (Col 3:8). That old way of thinking that revolved around ME, when I wanted MY WILL and MY WAY. That SELFISH thinking that, when it didn't get its way, was so prone to anger, wrath, malice, blasphemy, filthy communication out of my mouth, and lying (Col 3:8-9). Oh God, that was the OLD ME, and again, I put OFF all of the 'ME, MY, MINE' type of thinking and living today!

"But, I know that old residue of SELF that still lurks in this body of flesh (Rom

Chapter 10

7:23) is bound to try to crawl back up on the throne of my life today unless I PUT ON THE NEW MAN (Col 3:10-14). And Lord, at this very instant, I pour out all of ME to all of YOU, PUT OFF that OLD MAN, and submit and surrender myself to the fullness of who You are in my life. I willfully humble myself before you (1Pe 5:6) and pray that I will, indeed, PUT ON THE NEW MAN. That I may, indeed, PUT ON CHRIST (Gal 3:27) and all of those amazing and glorious characteristics that epitomized Your entire life — but especially the characteristics that brought You to the cross. All of those things that You had ON, that flowed out of you, and that brought me into this relationship with You and made me the NEW MAN (Col 3:10) that I am in You! May I have on today Your bowels of mercies, kindness, humbleness of mind, meekness, longsuffering, forbearance, forgiveness, and above all of these things, Your charity, which is the bond of perfectness (Col 3:12-14).

"And oh God, may the peace that You called me into when You reconciled me to Yourself (Col 1:20), may that PEACE reign in me today. Help me today to LET Your PEACE rule in my heart (Col 3:15). I pray that I won't allow my circumstances to rule me today — or anything but You for that matter! Not my nerves, my past, my present, my relationships — nothing but You, Lord, and Your PEACE (Col 3:15a). And with Your peace ruling, may I be THANKFUL today in every circumstance in which I find myself (Col 15b).

"And Lord, may I also LET You rule in me today through Your Word. May I LET the WORD of Christ dwell in me richly in all wisdom (Col 3:16). Oh, Lord, today may Your Word find entrance not only into my mind, but into every fabric of my entire being! May the word of Christ so control me today that it controls every word that comes out of my mouth (Col 3:17a). May every word that I speak be spoken in Your name today. I pray that nothing would come out of my mouth today that wouldn't come out of Yours! And I pray that every single deed that is done in my body today would likewise be done in Your name (Col 3:17b). May I not do anything in, through, or with this body today that You wouldn't do with Yours. I know I'm not my own (1Co 6:19). May I glorify You in my body and my spirit, which are Yours (1Co 6:20). Lord, I pray that my entire life today will be offered back to You as an expression of my gratitude to You for all that You are and all that You've done. Receive it as my offering of THANKSGIVING (Col 3:17c)."

Now, let me ask you… if that were the sincere, passionate, fervent (James 5:16b) prayer of our hearts, what do you think the answer to that prayer would look like as we carried out our respective roles in our homes? What would the answer to that prayer look like as we carried out our role as an employee or employer?

May God help Colossians 3:1-17 to be the prayer of our hearts today and every other day of our lives until Christ comes and redeems these bodies.

Chapter 11

Not I, but Christ

As we continue to reflect on Colossians 3:1-17, let me remind you of God's main idea in this incredible chapter. God is wanting to make sure that we understand that salvation wasn't merely "receiving Christ into our life." Oh, I know we use that terminology a lot, but I'm afraid it misses the real point! Salvation is NOT when I "receive Christ into my life" — it is when Christ BECOMES my life! And that is so much more than semantics! Let me say it another way: salvation is not merely a matter of ADDITION — it is a matter of TRANSFORMATION! Colossians 3:3-4a says,

> "For ye are dead, and your life is hid with Christ in God. When Christ, <u>who is our life</u>…"

We didn't just get Jesus deposited into our life! We died with Christ. We were buried with Him. And what came up out of the grave was something completely different than what went into it! We came out of the grave having been made NEW CREATURES in Christ (2Co 5:17). The way Paul refers to it in Colossians 3 is that we were made a NEW MAN (Col 3:9-10). And the implications cannot be underestimated.

You see, how we view our salvation has everything to do with how we approach our lives on the other side of that salvation. If I see it as ADDING Christ into my life, my life remains intact. I'm still the same old me, but now, because Jesus came into me, "I" resolve that "I" will do this for Him… "I" commit myself to Him… "I" am making Jesus Lord of my life… and on, and on, and on. Oh, do you hear the fallacy of those statements? I mean, don't those statements totally smack against everything that the New Testament teaches our salvation was and is? Man, I think the Apostle Paul would love

Chapter 11

to speak to us 21st-century folk about this whole matter! The crazy thing is, he wouldn't need to say anything different than what the Holy Spirit of God used him to say to first-century folk! I mean, can't you hear him say to us in 1 Corinthians 6:19-20...

> "What? Know ye not that your body is the temple of the Holy Ghost which is in you, which ye have of God, and <u>ye are not your own</u>? For <u>ye are bought</u> with a price: therefore glorify God in your body, and in your spirit, <u>which are God's</u>."

I almost feel like I hear him saying, "Didn't you guys understand what God was saying through me in Galatians 2:20?"

> "<u>I am crucified with Christ</u>: nevertheless I live [in other words, I still have physical life]; yet not I, <u>but Christ liveth in me</u>: and the life which I now live in the flesh I live by the faith <u>of</u> the Son of God, who loved me, and gave himself for me."

Are you catching what he's saying? In other words, salvation was our crucifixion and death. And yes, we still have a physical body that at this point is still alive, but now it is Christ who is actually the One living in us, because we're dead! And now it is not even a matter of us living FOR Jesus by OUR faith! No, Galatians 2:20 says that it isn't even OUR faith! Christ living IN and THROUGH us is by the faith OF Christ! Oh my, what a paradigm shift concerning the Christian life!

That little word "OF" is probably the most significant and telling word of that entire verse! And it isn't just a random word! Do you realize that God uses it every time He addresses the issue of what the Christian life is all about? Check out Philippians 3:9...

> "And be found in him, not having <u>mine own righteousness</u>, which is of the law, but that which is <u>through the faith of Christ</u>, the righteousness which is of God by faith:"

Whose faith — YOURS or Christ's? Well, since we're DEAD and He IS OUR LIFE, and it's Him LIVING in us, it must be HIS! He lives the Christian life THROUGH us, not by OUR faith — but HIS! The faith OF Christ!

And how about Romans 3:22?

"Even the righteousness of God which is by faith <u>of</u> Jesus Christ unto all and upon all that believe:"

Do you see how backwards our thinking can become about the Christian life? I mean, I know it sounds very spiritual to say, "Jesus died for me, and now, by my faith, I am going to live for Him." As spiritual as that may sound, I'm afraid our brother Paul would tell us that it is the very essence of the CARNAL MIND! Oh my, I know that sounds so strong and foreign to 21st-century "Christianity," but it is the clear teaching of Scripture!

Let me say it as succinctly and as clearly as I know how to say it: the Christian life is not about you LIVING FOR GOD. It is about you recognizing your DEATH and allowing CHRIST — in all of His fullness — TO LIVE THROUGH YOU! Look at 2 Corinthians 5:15…

"And that he died <u>for</u> all, that they which live should not henceforth live <u>unto themselves</u>, but <u>unto</u> him which died <u>for</u> them, and rose again."

This is the essence of Christianity! This is the reality that God keeps working to bring us to! Look at 2 Corinthians 4:10…

"Always bearing about in the body the dying of the Lord Jesus, that the <u>life</u> also <u>of Jesus</u> might be made <u>manifest in our body</u>."

The New Testament is so consistent about this! And the reason I'm so passionate about this is because this is where I think we allow the sorry devil to run us amok in the Christian life. Colossians 3 teaches us that when we came to Christ, we became a NEW MAN (or WOMAN). Not just a man with a new set of values, or a new way of thinking, or a new motivation for living… no! We were made a NEW MAN! Because Christ is now living IN us and THROUGH us!

What Colossians 3:1-17 is actually revealing to us is what the LIFE of CHRIST being lived THROUGH the NEW MAN actually looks like. Then, in 3:18-21, God shows us what the LIFE of Christ being lived THROUGH the NEW MAN looks like in the HOME. Then, in 3:22-4:1, He shows us what the LIFE of CHRIST being lived THROUGH the NEW MAN looks like in the WORKPLACE.

Chapter 11

And I think God is trying to get us to see that if we really have been made new creatures in Christ — if we really are a NEW MAN or a NEW WOMAN... if we truly are born again... the proof of it isn't going to be what we are at church. Man, all of us look so spiritual there — praying our prayers, singing the songs, saying amen, acting all reverent, speaking Christianese, wearing our Christian clothes. And all of that's fine, but it proves nothing! The proof of whether we're really a NEW MAN is who we are at HOME and who we are at WORK! That's where the real us comes out! All someone would have to do to find out if we're for real or to find out whether we're really allowing Christ's life to be lived through us is talk to our spouse and our children, and our boss and our coworkers.

I guess the point I'm trying to get you to see today is that this whole thing about having a new passion for God is, first and foremost, about having a new attitude about what salvation is! It's not about us exercising a massive dose of self-discipline, suppressing what we're really thinking and feeling, TRYING to be good Christians at work, or displaying good "Christian" attitudes. It'll just be a matter of time before the flesh gets unbelievably tired of trying to generate "Christ-like" behavior and reveals itself for what it really is! (It's amazing how STRONG the flesh can get when it gets TIRED!)

We're not our own (1Co 6:20). We don't even have a life to live today (Gal 2:20, Col 3:3). He hasn't called us to live FOR Him. He has called us to RECKON (to live in the practical reality of our position in Christ) ourselves to be DEAD indeed unto sin, but alive unto God through Jesus Christ our Lord (Rom 6:11). He's called us to YIELD ourselves to the reality of our DEATH to SELF and to our LIFE in and through CHRIST (Rom 6:13) and allow Him to just be who He is when we go to minister today. He wants the NEW MAN in us to serve today. So, let's get out of the way today and let the RISEN LIFE OF CHRIST in us find its full expression through us!

Four words from Galatians 2:20 sum up the mentality we need to have for every aspect of the Christian life:

"Not I, but Christ."

Four words from Galatians 5:16 sum it up just as simply and powerfully...

"Walk in the Spirit."

Remember, we don't live like God's people did in the Old Testament. God isn't just on the outside telling us how to live a holy life. He moved to the inside of us so HE can live out that holy life through our body. Oh, God, help me to get that! Oh, God, help us to get that!

Chapter 12

Better Off Dead

We learned from Colossians 3:1-2 that now that we're risen with Christ, we are to seek something different than we used to seek. Whereas in our B.C. (Before Christ) days we lived our lives seeking the things of this world (Eph 2:2-3, 1Jo 2:16, Col 3:7), we are now to live our lives seeking those things which are above (Col 3:1) in that realm where we are seated with Christ in heavenly places (Eph 2:6). We've taken the time together to biblically identify what those "things above" actually are and what God intended when He commanded us to set our affection on those things above (Col 3:2).

I hope you've taken hold of all that! We'll never hit the target if we don't know where to aim! Colossians 3:1-17 isn't stuff we can ever afford to move away from. The things God reveals to us in this passage are the things that daily RENEW OUR PASSION for the Lord and allow us to live in a "first love" kind of relationship with Him (Rev 2:4). It is that PASSION for Christ (3:1-17) that fuels us to carry out our responsibilities in all of our relationships: with our family (3:18-21), with our co-workers and employers (3:22-4:1), with the lost world (4:2-6), and with the body of Christ (4:7-18).

We've learned that we are to SEEK…

- The PERSON of God (1Jo 5:7), because God wants us to LOVE Him (Mark 12:30)
- The WORD of God (Psa 119:89), because God wants us to KNOW Him (Psa 27:8, Php 3:10, 1Jo 2:13-14, Psa 138:2)
- The THRONE of God (Eze 1:26-28, Isa 6:1, Rev 4), because God wants us to WORSHIP Him (John 4:23)

- The FAMILY of God (Eph 3:14-15), because God wants us to MINISTER through Him...
  - Our GIFTS to those IN His FAMILY (1Pe 4:10)...
  - And the GOSPEL to those He INTENDS to be in HIS FAMILY (Acts 20:24)

Oh yes, that is what God intends for us to PURSUE in life and what actually defines our PURPOSE in life, but we must factor one very significant thing into our understanding. If God's intention was simply that we LOVE Him and KNOW Him and WORSHIP Him and MINISTER through Him to those in His family, the absolute best thing God could have done — and I'm convinced <u>would</u> have done — is take us to heaven the very moment we called upon the name of the Lord to save us! Because the reality is, in heaven, we'll do all of those things better than we do now!

In heaven, we're going to LOVE Him more intimately than we do today. Because today, we still live in a body that hasn't yet experienced its redemption (Eph 1:14, Rom 8:23). It's a body that still has the remnants and residue of sin lodged in its members because of our life prior to receiving Christ (Rom 7:23). But, once we receive that glorified body (Php 3:21, Col 3:4), then we're going to love Him like we've never been able to love Him before! On that day, we will truly love Him with ALL of our heart, ALL of our soul, ALL of our mind, and ALL of our strength FOREVER!

In heaven, we'll also KNOW Him like we've never KNOWN Him before! 1 Corinthians 13:12 says, "For now we see through a glass, darkly; but then face to face: now I <u>know in part</u>; but then shall I <u>know</u> even as also I am <u>known</u>." Wow! When we get to Heaven, we'll know God as intimately as He knows us!

Not only will we LOVE Him more intimately and KNOW Him more fully, but in heaven, we'll also WORSHIP Him more passionately than we've ever worshipped Him before! If you want to get a taste of what our worship will be like as it comes forth out of a totally redeemed body, soul, and spirit, just check out Revelation 4. John has already been an eyewitness to those worshipping in redeemed bodies, worshipping in the fullness of what Jesus meant when He talked about "true worshippers" who worship "in spirit and in truth" (John 4:23).

So, when we get to heaven, we'll LOVE Him more intimately, KNOW Him more fully, and WORSHIP Him more passionately. And in terms of those who are already IN the FAMILY of God, realize this: they won't need us to MINISTER our GIFTS to them because they'll be LOVING, KNOWING, and WORSHIPPING Christ in the completeness and with the passion God intended, just like us.

There's just one thing that we won't do better in heaven than we can do right now. Do you know what it is? It is MINISTERING the GOSPEL to those God INTENDS to be in His FAMILY! And do you know why we can't do that better in heaven? Because there aren't any lost people there — and there will never be any lost people in heaven to minister the gospel to for all of eternity. It is the one thing that we MUST do now because we CANNOT do it in eternity! And THAT is the one reason that God has left us on this planet: to reach people with the gospel!

That's not to de-emphasize LOVING the Lord, KNOWING Him, or WORSHIPPING Him. A thousand times, NO! Those things certainly factor into our rewards at the judgment seat, and the truth is that the only people who are truly effective in MINISTERING the GOSPEL are those who do it from the platform of a life that LOVES Christ, KNOWS Him, and WORSHIPS Him. But the point I'm trying to make in all of this today is this…

If we are not going to fulfill God's purpose in leaving us on this planet — in other words, if we refuse or neglect to MINSTER the GOSPEL so that His FAMILY can grow to include more and more people who LOVE Him, and KNOW Him, and WORSHIP Him — the fact is: we'd be better off dead!

Now, look. I don't say that to get a reaction. I don't say that to sound uncaring, cold, or harsh. I say that because it's the honest gospel truth! If that's the one reason we're still here and we refuse to carry out that commission, He might as well take us to heaven now so we'll at least LOVE Him more intimately, KNOW Him more fully, and WORSHIP Him more passionately! To put it out there as plainly as I know how to put it, ministering the gospel is the only real reason we can justify our presence on this planet.

Years ago now, I read an article titled "A Parable of the Fishless Fishermen" by John M. Drescher that rocked my world. I'll share it with you here:

Chapter 12

Now it came to pass that a group existed who called themselves fishermen. And lo, there were many fish in the waters all around. In fact, the whole area was surrounded by streams and lakes filled with fish. And the fish were hungry.

Week after week, month after month, and year after year these who called themselves fishermen met in meetings and talked about their call to fish, the abundance of fish, and how they might go about fishing. Year after year they carefully defined what fishing means, defended fishing as an occupation, and declared that fishing is always to be a primary task of fishermen.

Continually they searched for new and better methods of fishing and for new and better definitions of fishing. Further they said, "The fishing industry exists by fishing as fire exists by burning." They loved slogans such as, "Fishing is the task of every fisherman's club." They sponsored special meetings called "Fishermen's Campaigns" and "The Month for Fishermen to Fish." They sponsored costly nationwide and worldwide congresses to discuss fishing and to promote fishing and hear about all the ways of fishing such as the new fishing equipment, fish calls, and whether any new bait was discovered.

These fishermen built large, beautiful buildings called "Fishing Headquarters." The plea was that everyone should be a fisherman and every fisherman should fish. One thing they didn't do, however: they didn't fish.

In addition to meeting regularly, they organized a board to send out fishermen to other places where there were many fish. All the fishermen seemed to agree that what is needed is a board which could challenge fishermen to be faithful in fishing, and to promote the idea of fishing in faraway streams and lakes where many other fish of different colors lived.

Also, the board hired staffs and appointed committees and held many meetings to define fishing, to defend fishing, and to decide what new streams should be thought about. But the staff and committee members did not fish.

Large, elaborate, and expensive training centers were built whose original and primary purpose was to teach fishermen how to fish. Over the years, courses were offered on the needs of fish, the nature of fish, where to find fish, the psychological reactions of fish, and how to approach and feed fish. Those who taught had doctorates in fishology. But the teachers did not fish. They only taught fishing. Year after year, after tedious training, many were graduated and were given fishing licenses. They were sent to do full-time fishing, some to distant waters which were filled with fish.

Some spent much study and travel to learn the history of fishing and to see faraway places where the founding fathers did great fishing in the centuries past. They lauded the faithful fishermen of years before who handed down the idea of fishing.

Further, the fishermen built large printing houses to publish fishing guides. Presses were kept busy day and night to produce materials solely devoted to fishing methods, equipment, and programs to arrange and to encourage meetings to talk about fishing. A speakers' bureau was also provided to schedule special speakers on the subject of fishing.

Many who felt the call to be fishermen responded. They were commissioned and sent to fish. But like the fishermen back home they never fished. Like the fishermen back home they engaged in all kinds of other occupations. They built power plants to pump water for fish and tractors to plow new waterways. They made all kinds of equipment to travel here and there to look at fish hatcheries. Some also said they wanted to be part of the fishing party, but they felt called to furnish fishing equipment. Others felt their job was to relate to the fish in a good way so the fish would know the difference between good and bad fishermen. Others felt that simply letting the fish know they were nice, land-loving neighbors and how loving and kind they were was enough.

After one stirring meeting on "The Necessity for Fishing," one young fellow left the meeting and went fishing. The next day he reported he had caught two outstanding fish. He was honored for his excellent catch and scheduled to visit all the big meetings possible to tell how he did it. So he quit his fishing in order to have time to tell about the experience to the other fishermen. He was also placed on the Fishermen's General Board as a person having considerable experience.

Now it's true that many of the fishermen sacrificed and put up with all kinds of difficulties. Some lived near the water and bore the smell of

Chapter 12

dead fish every day. They received the ridicule of some who made fun of their fishermen's clubs and the fact that they claimed to be fishermen yet never fished. They wondered about those who felt it was of little use to attend the weekly meetings to talk about fishing. After all, were they not following the Master who said, "Follow me, and I will make you fishers of men?"

Imagine how hurt some were when one day a person suggested that those who didn't catch fish were really not fishermen, no matter how much they claimed to be. Yet it did sound correct. Is a person a fisherman if year after year he never catches a fish? Is one following if he isn't fishing?

Oh, I beg you to consider this parable. Our Laodicean hearts so often deceive us into thinking we are passionate ministers of the gospel, and yet all we're doing is TALKING about being passionate about the gospel. We pat ourselves on the back for being "radical" about the book, but never actually get off our behinds and preach the good news of Christ's death, burial, and resurrection to the lost around us. There's no amount of Bible school, church camps, or even missions conferences (all potentially wonderful things!) that can let us be called fishermen — only getting out there and FISHING can earn us that title!

As we're seated up there in heaven with Christ and His family, He desires that as we're walking down here on earth, we see those people that we work with, that we go to school with, that we're friends with, that we're neighbors with, that we're related to, as people who our loving Father wants to be in His family. And from the platform of a child of God whose life is passionately pursuing Him, He desires that we go through our life each day praying, "Lord, help me as I go to work, as I'm in my neighborhood. Open doors for me to minister the gospel to those You want to see seated with us in heavenly places." If we're not going to do this with our lives, I really do believe we'd be better off dead!

May I remind you that the things we've discussed throughout this book aren't the "deeper" Christian life, but rather the very basics of it? The passage we've been focusing on is, I believe, God's outline for how He wants us to live this RISEN LIFE we now have in Christ. My friends, I so desperately desire that each of us would have a life which others could proclaim lines up with God's outline in Colossians 3 and 4.

As we tie a bow on things, may I ask you a few questions?

How does your life line up with the seven key verbs in Colossians 3:1-17? Namely...

Are you SEEKING and SETTING YOUR AFFECTION on the things above? On the PERSON of God because you desire to LOVE Him, on the WORD of God because you desire to KNOW Him, on the THRONE of God because you desire to WORSHIP Him, and on the FAMILY of God because you desire to MINISTER through Him?

Are you MORTIFYING the desires of your flesh?

Are you PUTTING OFF the old man and PUTTING ON the new man which is renewed through God's word?

Are you LETTING the peace of God rule in your heart, or are you LETTING other people, emotions, or circumstances do so?

Are you LETTING the word of Christ dwell in you richly in all wisdom, thereby walking in the Spirit?

Could those around you — your spouse, kids, coworkers, friends, church family — honestly say that these things are true about you?

If so, praise God! May you continue to walk on earth like you're seated in heaven until our faith is made sight! But if you find yourself lacking (as we all will at one time or another!), simply reflect on the truths we've seen from God's word. Remember that you haven't LOST your first love, but rather LEFT it — and it can be found! Hunger to be hungry. Thirst to be thirsty. May you soon return to that first love and find yourself fully restored in the joy of your salvation (Psa 51:12).

Would to God that each of us take such a firm hold of God's principles in Colossians that we arrive at the judgment seat of Christ having passionately pursued Him until the day He took us home.

Made in the USA
Coppell, TX
18 May 2024

32517703R10049